# CATCH, RELEASE

D0217710

Johns Hopkins: Poetry and Fiction

Wyatt Prunty, *General Editor*

# CATCH, RELEASE

Stories by ADRIANNE HARUN

Johns Hopkins University Press    Baltimore

This book has been brought to publication with the generous assistance
of the John T. Irwin Poetry and Fiction Endowed Fund.

Johns Hopkins University Press
2715 North Charles Street
Baltimore, Maryland 21218-4363
www.press.jhu.edu

Library of Congress Cataloging-in-Publication Data

Names: Harun, Adrianne, author.
Title: Catch, release : stories / by Adrianne Harun.
Description: Baltimore : Johns Hopkins University Press, 2018. | Series:
    Johns Hopkins: poetry and fiction
Identifiers: LCCN 2018004458 | ISBN 9781421426693 (paperback :
    acid-free paper) | ISBN 1421426692 (paperback : acid-free paper) |
    ISBN 9781421426709 (electronic) | ISBN 1421426706 (electronic)
Classification: LCC PS3608.A788 A6 2018 | DDC 813/.6—dc23
    LC record available at https://lccn.loc.gov/2018004458

A catalog record for this book is available from the British Library.

*Special discounts are available for bulk purchases of this book.*
*For more information, please contact Special Sales at 410-516-6936 or*
*specialsales@press.jhu.edu.*

Johns Hopkins University Press uses environmentally friendly book
materials, including recycled text paper that is composed of at least 30
percent post-consumer waste, whenever possible.

*For my dear ones: Ali, Duncan, Peter, and Bailey*

# CONTENTS

# CATCH, RELEASE

# LOST IN THE WAR OF THE BEAUTIFUL LADS

A waif-like soldier of the teenage wars, Corrie was never without her backpack. It was stuffed with the midriff-baring sweaters that I didn't like, as well as makeup and an abundance of iconic offerings she kept for new friends: fragile worry dolls, stippled beach rocks, a henna tattoo kit. And her cigarettes, a silver lighter from an old boyfriend, hair clips shaped like butterflies and set with fake gems. Gum, pencils, tissues. Startlingly, a change of underwear. When the RCMP handed it back to me, Corrie's belongings were organized neatly—as neatly, at least, as if she had packed them all herself. In other words, untouched.

Three kids in a pickup truck. In a field. Corrie in the middle, her head on a shoulder, another leaning against her. The three of them like a trio of knocked-over pins. One window shattered. Glass on their laps. An empty open CD case on Garrett's knee. Corrie's hand clutching a wilted moss rose so tightly the woody stem had split, leaving a thin gash across her tender palm.

Just three kids out for a ride, listening to music, maybe firing up a blunt, although the ashtray was closed, no matches in any of their pockets. That lighter of Corrie's way down at the bottom of the pack. No bottles either. Just the music, the flower, the broken glass, a bullet each, and no one else disturbed.

May Shannon, my neighbor, commiserated: "You might expect it in a city, even a school or a fast food joint, the bowling alley—but a field, on an island no less." I knew what she meant. You couldn't help seeing circles in your mind: tight, impenetrable. One forgets about

< 1 >

implosions. The three of them in the center, the field beyond, the island shore and surf ringing them all. And my daughter Corrie, the bull's-eye. It's not true that no one in Canada keeps guns. Someone here had, for instance. A .45 fired at close range. And only the one ferry, arriving and departing like the tide.

*Enemies?* the police asked us. *Strange characters lurking about?*

Well, what did they expect us to say to *that?*

It's no secret that, put anywhere else, most of us on the island would appear odd. Last year, I went down to Vancouver on my yearly shopping trip. I was scanning the racks at The Bay, bowled over more by the other customers than by the merchandise. So much affluence, so young. I had no place there. I was too old and foreign and my intentions weren't honorable. I would not under any circumstances buy a tiny leather skirt or a sleeveless cashmere sweater. Not even for Corrie. I wanted a winter coat, something just slightly more refined than the usual island wear. Apparently what I was searching for did not exist. I could sew one easily, I supposed, but sewing was what I did for a living, and this trip was a chance to treat myself. I half-heartedly considered a quilted white parka with a fur collar. Ridiculous, a white jacket, meant only for a rich twitch to wear out to dinner at the ski resort. I would dirty it beyond repair just climbing into the truck. Yet there I was, holding out a sleeve, stroking the collar, when a bag lady crept beside me. I saw scraggling gray-blond hair, shabby mismatched clothing, sweaters over sweaters, brown tie-up shoes the worse for wear. The first flash, that. Then in the next instant the bag lady was Helly from the island. Helly with her big pink flower satchel. Helly at The Bay! We exclaimed; we, who hardly spoke to each other at home, had lunch together. She showed me a lipstick she'd bought. I opened the box containing my new boots. In the mirror behind our restaurant booth, I saw us as we must have appeared to others: two ragged people, friends with uneasy full wallets, waiting for the waitress to grace us with her attention. Helly was going on to visit a sister. I hadn't even known she had a sister. After lunch, I accompanied her to the bus stop, watched her revert from Helly back into the bag lady as she hauled her bundles up the steep bus steps behind two young girls in identical black sweaters and black leather skirts.

And that was only Helly. We have far odder folks on the island.

Blunt Bob, the marijuana farmer. Ashley, the broad-shouldered transsexual, who quite possibly lives in a cave off Whittle Beach. The Samuelsons in their yurt complex. Our hermit, who lives in the exact center of the island and has his groceries delivered to a red plastic crate by the abandoned logging road. And don't forget the ex-Navy commander who gives palm readings and who sometimes becomes hysterical when we pick plums and wild strawberries in the metal-strewn lots behind his trailer.

Corrie went to him last year for a reading. My own idea of a birthday present for a fourteen-year-old who thought she knew everything.

In the cramped stall of his trailer, the white-haired commander sat stiffly beside her. He took her left hand as if he might bow and kiss it. He held it out in front of him and squinted, then brought it close to him, turning her palm upward. With one finger he traced the six major lines on her palm, gave them names: *Heart, Head, Life, Mercury, Apollo, Saturn.* Her hand, he pronounced, was conical, the fingers long and knotted. He deciphered the crosses and stars and little hashes that marked her palm. He clucked over the feathery lines, the presence or absence of "padding." Declared, without irony, with surprise even, that Corrie had a heart. She preened, smirked at me a little. The commander bristled when he saw that.

"Listen up," he said, sternly. "This isn't a prize, girl." He dragged long and hard on his hand-rolled cigarette, letting the smoke escape slowly as he continued. "Having a heart," he smiled, showing a mouthful of long, yellow teeth, "just means that you can be stopped."

He offered to read my palm as well, but the truth is, since I moved to the island just before Corrie was born, my own future has been clear enough. And I certainly had no desire to be called down for my failings. (Corrie was already doing a fine job of that, thank you.) Besides, despite his pressed exterior, the old man's hands were filthy, stained by cigarettes and fruit pulp, and his fly was half-unzipped. I couldn't wait to get out of that musty trailer, rank with the smell of nesting rats and rotting plums.

Before we left, he drew my daughter toward a tiny copy machine on his kitchen counter.

"Oh, yes, just like that," he breathed, pressing her hand tightly over the flashing roll of light.

I expected him to offer us the copy; my hand was open for it. Instead, he slipped the blackened image of Corrie's hand into a flesh-colored folder.

"It's mine," he said, pushing the door open for us. "Who knows what I'll see here in the future."

———————

Over the phone, May Shannon tells me there are investigators on island. They've visited her, promised to visit everyone. They are probably listening right now over the party line, getting a feel for who we are and how we conduct our business. She giggles a little at the thought that we are all suspect, then immediately apologies. "It's not funny," she says. "I don't know why I'm laughing." Nothing makes sense, I want to say, why should this? She's whispering now, asking if I've been out to the field. It's on my way to the beach, she knows, the beach where I usually clam. Never mind that I don't clam during this cold windy season. She makes us sound like conspirators, and maybe it's that, maybe it's because they might be listening, that I pretend fear. "Do they think we're safe?" I ask May. The silence that meets my unexpected question tells me that May has never thought of this herself. Has never wondered if another murder will follow this inexplicable one. Such is not the way we think here on island.

---

And then we have the funerals. They are almost too much for us to bear. Three in a row. One boy's family is Catholic. They take him to the mainland, and we all go down to the ferry and see him off. Garrett's family, although not churchgoers, has a service in the Methodist church, the only real church on the island, a sweet gray clapboard chapel close to the beach. For Corrie, my partner Jasper and I forgo a formal funeral. Instead, we rent the kitchen shelter in the provincial park. Jasper's idea. He's the one with all the ideas now, although when we had Corrie here, he was clueless, always retreating to the studio when Corrie and I batted heads.

"She's your daughter," he said when I asked for help.

Yet Jasper and Corrie sometimes seemed more kin than she and I did, the way they each burrowed away from me at times, reveling in solitude and secret projects.

At the kitchen shelter, we serve high tea, Corrie's favorite. As a little girl, she loved to linger around the lobby of the Empress Hotel in Victoria, hoping we'd come up with the thirty dollars a head to treat her to high tea. We never did. So we have it now. We choke down scones and Devon cream, little sandwiches smeared with salmon paste or chopped egg. May Shannon's husband, Ed, keeps a flask of whiskey handy and doctors my tea each time I hand the cup round for a refill.

---

The Vancouver police find Corrie's fake ID on a runaway. The runaway insists a boyfriend got it for her, but—surprise!—the boyfriend is nowhere to be found.

"They all vanish," I mutter to Jasper as my eyes close that night. I hardly hear his answer. I used to be the one awake until dawn, charged with dread, as I listened for her. Now, for what seems like the first time in two years, I collapse deeply, astonished each morning by the calm autumn sun warming my face.

After the first shock and tumult dies down, our neighbor, the hermit, brings us a Bundt cake on a chipped china plate rimmed with hand-painted forget-me-nots. He unlaces his muddy boots at the door—one filthy hand balancing on the doorsill, the other bearing the teetering plate—and sidles into the living room. He stays to eat two pieces himself, expressing a querulous preference for the Hawaiian Kona coffee we once gave him over the cinnamon tea Corrie favored and which still crams a cupboard shelf. A narrow-faced, gray-haired man with bloodshot eyes, he looks as if he's been weeping. Once he has his coffee and cake, he might as well be alone, so fierce is his concentration. Even when we lay our forks down on our empty plates, we have nothing to say. But our old Lab, Pamela, who's been pining for Corrie for ages, likes the hermit, and he wrestles with her on the living room floor until the coffee table topples to the rug. A blue pottery dish filled with beach glass is upset. Tears fill the hermit's eyes as he apologizes, scurrying around on his hands and knees to pinch up the pieces before he flees.

---

One of the boys, the Catholic one, Danny, had a record on the mainland. He stole parts from cars, they tell us, and, worse, hustled sex-starved tourists at the Granville market. Not uncommon, we're told. There's a cadre of lost children, boys mostly, who survive in the city this way. But Danny did not live in the city and whether his past plays into the *incident*—as the police call it—is still not certain. I imagine a thug fondling young Danny against a wall while demanding a missing carton of hubcaps. I shake my head. Always, these days I'm shaking my head.

---

The local newspaper prints Corrie's yearbook picture. It's the first time I've seen it because the proofs had gone right to the school, and no one wanted to upset us by sending them over. She's unbearably beautiful in her photograph, even in the grainy newspaper reproduction. Her sometimes spotty skin has been smoothed. Her hair shines; her smile is without guile. She is our bright toddler brought to fruition. None of the painful transformation, the awful twisting of our girl into the screaming wretch she'd become in the past year—none of that visible at all. Not for the first time, I wonder if there's been a mistake, if the girl in the truck was a genuine stranger, perhaps someone Corrie befriended at school.

The island school is just for little kids. Come high school, we put the children on a boat every morning and send them to a bigger island where they meet children we'll never know, like Corrie's supposed friend Alicia. Two weeks after the funerals, Alicia reveals a skimpy diary in which Corrie, in an unfamiliar rounded hand, blames her father, my ex, Kenneth, for unspeakable injuries. In the diary, she details her plans to leave for Vancouver. Money, she insinuates, is no problem. An unbearable excitement throbs behind her proclamations that no one will believe how easily she disappears, how her tracks will be so well hidden even Pamela couldn't sniff them out. I find myself rooting for her, whispering words I could never say when she was here. *Go ahead,* I urge as I read a supposed entry for September 22, *leave. Hurry, sweetheart, hurry.* The only mention of me comes in the last paragraph of the diary when she writes: *My mother will have no problem renting my room. She's always said she could get big money for a room by the beach.*

Of course this isn't true. Likely none of the journal is true. Kenneth has lived in Toronto since Corrie was a year old and does not, to this day, acknowledge his part in our glorious girl. I found a number for him and left a message on his machine right after the RCMP came, but he never called back. If Corrie has seen him in recent years, it has only been in her dreams. Our house, by the way, is a mile and a half from the beach in a meadow, bordered by an alder-choked clear-cut and a field full of purple thistles. Jasper and I couldn't even find a summer renter for the studio we made in the barn, and studios, as you may know, are in great demand here.

---

Weeks pass and the investigation peters out, although that's not what they tell us. A Mountie stops by one evening to give us an update. I have one of my bad headaches and have to leave the room to vomit. He stays, sipping coffee with Jasper for almost an hour while I lie in our loft bed, feeling the murmur of their voices spin through the floorboards and into the relentless glare from the skylight. Afterwards, Jasper only remembers how heavily the man sugared his coffee and how he assured Jasper every few minutes that they would leave no stone unturned. If he asked questions, Jasper isn't repeating them.

"Lynnie, you know they're doing their best," he tells me, averting his eyes from my incredulous stare.

What does that mean—*their best?* *Best* is shining A+, gold star, a tiny girl twirling into my arms on the beach, squealing, *Look, Mum, I made a new country*, as she pulls me toward her deep sand hole with clamshells set around as tidy houses, exactly mimicking our island geography. *Best* is not a thin-lipped Mountie, emptying the sugar bowl. When Jasper leaves for his studio, I spill the sugar into the trash and slam the pottery bowl against the wall. Afterwards, I

<8>

can almost hear Corrie's slow, mocking applause, the door slamming behind her.

———————

Nearly five more months go by. The Catholic family leaves the island. Garrett's mum, Betty, has back surgery in Vancouver and doesn't return for weeks. His dad takes up with May Shannon's little sister, Charlotte, and when Betty returns, it's to an empty house. Except for May, I don't speak with any of them any more, not even when we bump into each other in the aisles of the Co-op. I want to burrow out of sight, putting a vast distance between me and their grasping shared condolences. I leave it to Jasper to nod, pass the slightest of pleasantries. He's good at that, too, I've noticed lately.

Staying on the surface, I mean.

———————

The seasons change; you can't stop them. Jasper spends all day and some of each night in the barn studio, readying his pottery for the summer fair circuit. He specializes in oblong platters glazed with swirling sea-greens and blues. Lately, the platters have grown ominously heavy, gaining in length and breadth as well. When they're finished, he wraps them in thin swathes of styrofoam, covers that with layers of newspaper, and stacks them in his van. More than once, I've been startled by the sight of him, hoisting his shrouded platters across the drive.

The week before Jasper leaves, my father comes to visit from Victoria where he runs a whale touring business. It's his busy season, the spring migration underway, but somehow he's managed to get away. When he hugs me, I feel myself shatter and reassemble in a new, sturdier form. He can steady you, Dad can. Once, when I was a child and we were camping up in the Kootenays, I saw him set a hiker's broken leg into a splint. He had to twist the leg to set it straight. His hands were calm and quick and the hiker, a banker from Richmond, never even cried out. The man sent us Christmas cards for years.

Dad has always been a fastidious eater. At dinner, he would insist upon separating his food into non-touching piles and would eat one small heap entirely before approaching the next. It's a habit he says he picked up in the army, eating off mess trays. Spoonful after spoonful of peas, followed by neatly cut-up pieces of browned beef, then the roasted new potatoes, whole on the fork. Corrie always admired his habit. For a few miserable months, she imitated him. It was a bone of contention between us. I remember the night I'd had enough of her picking tiny bits of onion and corn from her rice and placing them in separate piles beside the already segregated chicken. I went a little crazy. I dove into her plate myself, swirling vegetables and rice and chicken together, dumping spoonfuls of chutney and pineapple into the mix. Then I did something far more shaming: I picked up a spoon and began forcing the mess into her nine-year-old mouth, even as she wept and wailed and the food dribbled over her face and chest. Remembering, I take myself off to the bathing shed Jasper built where I switch on the bumptious whirlpool and try to slow my heart to the marching beat of the pump.

At supper on the first night of Dad's visit, I place three separate plates in front of my father and force myself to observe his routine. Jasper chastises me with a look that says I'm being rude, but Dad isn't offended. During his two-day visit, he is careful with me, accepting every suggestion I make without a single complaint. We walk the beach. I measure him for a new shirt I'll make. At night, we go out to the café by the ferry dock and drink beer while we watch the lights on the water, the otters playing around the dock pilings. He doesn't say a word about Corrie's backpack, which I carry everywhere these days. Before my father leaves, Jasper exhibits his new platters for him, and I make a lame joke about taking one along on one of his off-season whale tours. Neither Jasper nor my father finds my joke funny. I laugh so hard my eyes tear and my chest ratchets with pain. My father presses my arm too tightly.

"Lynnie," he says, as if he's been waiting years to get my attention, "You need to get out of here."

For the first time in my life, I shrug him off roughly, shake my head with a sour smile. I can never leave here now. Jasper at least knows that much. He hasn't even hinted that I should come along this year for the three months he spends going around mainland craft fairs. Last summer we decided we would plant a crop of Lasqueti bud in the back field, but this doesn't seem a good idea anymore, despite the unbelievable prices Blunt Bob is getting. Instead, a few weeks earlier than necessary, Jasper packs his van and offers me a dry, painful kiss goodbye.

––––––––––

Keep busy, the island widows advised me at Corrie's memorial tea. I pick early strawberries and scavenge downed plums behind the ex-Navy commander's trailer, ignoring the trenches lined with wire fencing that he's dug around the trees, ostensibly to keep the likes of me away. I grab my rake and shovel and bucket and pass through the field to the beach. It's part of my routine now, this clamming. May Shannon says she doesn't know how I do it. She'd be terrified. As if the killer is still there, a part of the field, an island ghost like my girl. I don't tell May about her little red boots still in the mudroom or the childish clam rake leaning beside mine. How when my girl was little she'd run along the beach, stamping at the clam holes, squealing when the clam would spit, that jet of water always taking her by surprise, no matter how many times I explained that every wild thing—even a clam—needs to protect itself. I don't tell May how I scolded Corrie, how I was impatient, how I did not listen—ever, it seems—to her joy or her need.

———————

Island children are such pretty children, have I mentioned that? Ruddy-cheeked, dressed in brilliant scraps of homemade clothes, they own the island with their hidden forts and meandering bicycles, their restless, concentrated wonder. They are the best of us, those little ones, the reason so many of us came here in the first place: to give our beautiful children a life outside the world. It didn't occur to us then how we carry the terrors of civilization within us.

In late spring, the island school hires me to make one of those huge parachutes they use in the primary school to teach cooperation. I remember this from Corrie's time. All the students in a circle, holding tightly to their bit of parachute silk. Together, they loft the parachute over and over again into the air until, on the count of three, they simultaneously duck their heads inside. If they all work together, it's a seamless, selfless motion. Supposedly, this swell of togetherness will etch in their communal memories and keep them from harming each other as they grow older.

The parachute is always a big hit. The children adore the moment when the ordinary disappears into a prism of darting color and light, and they giggle madly, knowing the adults will wait for them to reappear. But the last time they tried to hoist the ratty old parachute, the fabric tore, leaving a few forlorn children outside the circle, their hands full of unraveled silk. One child, half-visible, began to sob. The school secretary telephoned me that afternoon.

I have all the pieces cut out and pieced and am sewing on the machine when the hermit arrives with an another Bundt cake—this one, chocolate-swirled, with cocoa sifted prettily over the top. The entire living room is strewn with lengthy diamond-shaped panels of parachute silk. I have them hanging from the loft railing, draped over the couch and the chairs. Strips of lemon yellow, fuchsia, azure, and chartreuse. More fabric bunched on my lap and slung around my shoulders: turquoise, orange, the reddest of reds. The hermit grins in awed relief. To him it must seem as if I'm wrapped up in happiness.

When Pamela sees the hermit from her banishment on the deck, she starts her whining. Her tail hits the barbecue grill, and the air behind her clouds with charcoal dust. The tender hermit abruptly grimaces, already blaming himself.

"It's all right," I tell him. "It's not your fault."

I'm out of coffee. Out of tea, as well, since Jasper took the last of Corrie's tea with him. No milk and only the last scummy bit of apple juice in a recycled gallon container. Even the filtered water barrel is nearly bone dry. I fling open one cabinet door after another, slam them all shut. Plates jump, glasses shiver. A salt cellar flips on its side and rolls under the refrigerator. I sink to the floor as if I'm about to rescue it, but all I can think of is how much I want to join it in the close dark. When I open my eyes, the hermit is still waiting. He's crouched across from me beside the sliding glass door with Pamela sprawled on the other side as if she's leaning into him.

"Come on, then," the hermit says. He pulls me awkwardly to my feet, hands me Corrie's backpack, and steers me to the door. His fingers feel like sandpaper.

Years ago, when I first arrived on the island and was fiercely walking my way through my pregnancy, I plunged onto the wrong trail and ended up hiking through a swampy marsh that led, I learned later, to the center of the island where the hermit lives. I remember telling this story to Corrie when she was six and liked to spend whole mornings hiding in a big cardboard box in the center of the kitchen. Corrie was intrigued. So, years after my first hike in his territory, we tried, without luck, to find the hermit's lair again. All we could see was a curved roof made out of mismatched roofing tiles with a crooked brick chimney in the center. A thicket of Himalayan blackberries made any further approach unthinkable. With my help, Corrie baked oatmeal cookies, and together we left them in the hermit's metal crate by the logging road. Corrie added a drawing she made of a little pink house with a smiling face filling a window. A few days after that, the hermit appeared at our door with the first of his cakes, although he wouldn't stay and his voice, that testy whine, frightened Corrie. Now the hermit leads me, with Pamela squeezing beside us, right into the brambles around his house. I pull back, yet he insists.

"There's a path," he says.

I don't see any path. Still, we barely scrape the first canes before we're in a fragrant tunnel in the midst of the blackberries but safely away from thorns. A moment later, we emerge into an expansive, sunny clearing, spinning with raised, double-dug garden beds. The hermit has shaped all his garden plots in spirals and rings, and the trail through them is equally dizzying. At the center is his house, just a shack really, covered, even this early in the season, with yellow and pink roses. I pride myself on my own flower garden, but I don't recognize any of the hermit's roses. If Corrie were here, she would shoulder past me into the cottage the hermit calls home. She would coo and exclaim until he reddened with embarrassment. Her fingers would stroke the quiet contours of his books, his surprisingly fussy knickknack shelf. A keepsake might slip unnoticed into her pocket.

The hermit motions me to stay in the yard. As he disappears into his cottage with Pamela wagging shamelessly beside him, I fold myself onto the grass and inhale. Purple sage is in bloom, the peas are flowering, and bulbs of garlic with their long green spikes still attached lie on a screen set up on four bricks.

The hermit presents me with a slice of cake on a china plate (this one rimmed with silver) and a shaking teacup filled to the brim with strong black coffee. Over his tattered sleeve, he's placed a single ivory-colored linen napkin, and he offers that to me as well. The fork is heavy and silver, and with each bite I feel pampered and reassured.

"Your roses," I begin, as if he's neglected an introduction. "I don't know their names."

I've heard that, years ago, the hermit was a university professor named Ewan Millet. We have books in the island library supposedly authored by that man, a historian. Now he jumps to his feet to snap off blooms and bring them to me with their stories. Here is the Yellow Noisette and the rosy-pink *Gracilis*.

"*Gracilis*," he says in a slightly pompous way that reminds me of May Shannon, "is a Boursault. This white, violet-scented beauty is a Banksia, named for the wife of Thomas Banks, who accompanied her husband on Captain Cook's ship, *Endeavor*, as it sailed around the world. Her kinfolk thought she had disappeared off the face of the earth."

His last offering is the least appealing: a rough purple blossom shot through with shades of crimson. He thrusts it into my hand, splashing coffee on the linen napkin.

"See," he crows as if I've challenged him, "no thorns. According to the followers of Zoroaster, roses had no thorns until the arrival of evil in the world."

"Zoroaster?" I say, but the hermit ignores me. He is too excited.

"Think of it," he says in his high, soft voice. "Something that knows no evil."

I have a sudden urge to pluck each unlovely petal from the rose:

introduce it to my world. The hermit doesn't seem to see my out-stretched hand. He tucks the rose—*alpina* he calls it—into Corrie's backpack. His stranger's hand emerging from the backpack reminds me of what the RCMP would not return to me.

"There are additional items, Mrs. Campbell," a Mountie had said, holding out a glass pipe with a pair of tubular stems and a wad of bills wrapped in the green flowered scarf I once saved in tissue for fancier potlucks. "Perhaps you recognize them?"

"I'm sorry," I said, shaking my head.

I caught her wearing the scarf as a halter. No big deal, perhaps, but it seemed monumental at the time, the way she sifted through my things, culling out the best, only to later trash or abandon each much-cared-for article. The scarf was already ruined. Burned along one hem. I don't even know why I wanted it back.

*Selfish bitch*, she called me, her face twisted with rage.

Again and again, she defied me. And why not? What did *I* under-stand of the world? Shut away here on the island.

*You're mine*, I told her. *That's all I need to know.*

*You don't know me at all*, she spat in return.

I chased her, catching the scorched hem of the scarf. I can feel it yet, the pinch of stiffened fabric pulling away.

---

At home, May Shannon is on the phone. She is astonished to hear I have been visiting the hermit, that I have had Bundt cake and coffee in his garden while he braided garlic and introduced me to his roses.

"He's crazy, Lynnie," she warns. "Aside from you, he hasn't been around people in twenty years, they say."

"Yeah, that's crazy all right," I tell May Shannon, laying the re-ceiver in its cradle and easing away from the window as an unfamiliar green car appears in the gravel driveway. The car comes to rest beside my old truck.

Used to be we would all perk up at the sight of a guest, but the woman who emerges from the green car, this woman in her navy skirt and sensible heels, chills me. She is obviously off-island, most likely a tourist following the hand-lettered sign Jasper posted on the main road to advertise his pottery studio.

But her name is Gayle Something-or-Other from the RCMP, and she has news for me about Corrie's friend Danny and the ex-Navy commander.

"Mrs. Campbell?" she says, when I finally come to the door. "Oh, I'm so glad I caught you at home."

———

All through the long afternoon, I work on the parachute. The sewing machine's lurch and rumble, its harsh whirring, mirrors something inside me. The needle pierces the fabric; seams are joined. Still, nothing fits quite right; the fabric puckers and gapes.

"Yes, Mrs. Campbell," Gayle had said when I challenged her. "We are absolutely certain." She went on to describe the commander's folders, the smudged sheets of photocopied hands, all foretelling a terrible end.

My fault. Corrie was right: In the end, I would be the one to blame.

At dusk, that splintered hour between day and night when I can half-hear her banging across the deck, I finally look up. Corrie's backpack slumps into a corner of the couch as if she threw it there herself. The graceful hand with its bitten-down nails and stained fingers lofting the backpack into the air, declaring her return. It occurs to me that I could see that hand again or, more accurately, I could see Corrie's fourteen-year-old hand. I could examine it myself.

———

< 17 >

The moment I round the corner to the ex-commander's trailer, the news Gayle Something-or-Other was so eager to share grows teeth, as Dad would say. The trailer is encircled by bright orange tape that hangs limply like the ribbon on an unwanted present. The tape won't keep me out, nor will the smell coming from the place. That same rank, fruity smell that worked its way into Corrie's hair the afternoon he told her fortune. My eyes are stinging as I pinch the meager lock, let myself inside, and switch on the naked bulbs this monster lived beneath.

"A casualty in the War of the Beautiful Lads," that's what Gayle said he called Corrie. A war for which he himself had been decades too late, one that he felt held his destiny.

"You check the evidence," he'd screamed when they came for him. "You'll see I had no choice."

They've gone through everything. The file cabinet where he kept his manila folders is missing. Its absence creates the only clean patch on the soiled dun-colored carpet. The tacky, wheezing copy machine has vanished, too. Still, it seems possible that the file with Corrie's handprint might have been overlooked. I open drawers and root gingerly through a cupboard. I can make out dusty gaps on the bookshelves—presumably places where the RCMP found suspect volumes. What remains are an odd mix of poetry and psychology books, a collection of essays by Walter Pater, and several much-read war biographies, one thick with illustrations that remind me of William Blake's hallucinations of Heaven and Hell.

The rage I feel at the missing handprint creeps upon me, arriving with a force that almost blows me apart. I rip through the trailer, up-ending the already torn-apart bench seats, smashing a bowl half-full of rotting plums. As the air fractures around me, a series of high-pitched strangling cries emerges without warning from my throat.

Eventually, I bang my hip hard against the aluminum edge of the

< 18 >

Formica table and collapse into the trailer's only chair, the one Corrie claimed that day. The ripped leatherette seat scrapes the back of my thighs. When I pick up one of the bad plums and squeeze it, the juice stings like crazy, and I notice the knuckles of my right hand are bleeding. This new pain seems almost pleasurable.

She lied, you know, more easily than she told the truth. She stole whatever she fancied, as well as the less desirable treasures of others. Her capacity for malice, too, transcended any hopes the rest of us harbored for her. Last summer, after Ed Shannon gave her a job registering overnight visitors at the boat haven, she chugged a pilfered half-liter of tequila and rampaged through the docks, breaking glass and swearing loudly, until a liveaboard used the pay phone at the laundromat to call Ed.

"You don't watch yourself, young lady, they'll have you locked in a box," he told her.

"As if I fucking care," she taunted him.

She would have gone anyway, and I would have grieved even as I dreaded her return. It's that tangled anticipation I won't have, I realize, the nights of pained wakefulness, the clench of our mutual disdain rasping against my hopes for her. No matter how far she roamed, she would still hover near enough to flail at the open, ever-deepening wounds she loved to inflict.

A salt breeze enters the trailer and mixes with the gassy mold of the trailer. I clutch Corrie's backpack to my chest to steady myself. As I do, my hand brushes against my mouth, the stink of my daughter's murderer lands on my tongue, and I am finally weeping, knowing that I am left with only this: a backpack full of childish longings, a daughter I can carry.

# THE FARMHOUSE WIFE

They had been searching for three weeks and were nearly desperate when they heard about the farmhouse. By then it didn't matter that the house was way out in the country, a good ten country miles from work. After four months camping in the state park, they were bone-tired. No matter how carefully they positioned the tent, each night new roots seemed to twine beneath their shoulders and into the small of their backs, the initial discomfort growing knobbier and more impossibly painful as the night went on. They were popping aspirin with the coffee they perked with eggshells over an open flame—for their backs and for the constant headaches, too, the result of the campground clientele's late-night romps. The weeknights weren't so bad, but the weekends were unbearable, with the usually empty campsites suddenly overwhelmed by loud families slouching in tattered lawn chairs. So predictable, that cacophony. The clash of blaring radios all tuned to different stations. Children fighting among themselves, then squalling as if their greatest treasures had been stolen, right there, that moment, in Lost Willows State Campground. Inevitably, cursing began at midnight. Festering arguments seemed to come alive in the confines of a tent or trailer, as if civilized behavior could only be maintained within proper walls.

"I feel so poor," Janis said. "As if we'll never get out of this, but just sink lower and lower until we're indistinguishable from dirt." She did feel dirty all the time. Walking back from the campground shower, her sandals filled with dust. She'd found twigs in her underwear. Her socks were always twisted and a little damp. Jimmy was in no better shape. He had big purplish welts on his stomach—from spider bites, they thought. And now the weather was growing colder. During this past week they'd been one of only three other groups of campers in the park, the others in heated trailers with electric lights and satellite dishes. Soon these, too, would be gone, and eventually even the weekend disasters would stay home.

Dreams of an in-town apartment had gone out the window first. If they spent every cent they made on rent, ate frugally, and hardly used their car, they believed their paychecks might stretch into a month's rent. They had nearly reconciled themselves to this and to other economies, such as stealing twisted bags of popcorn from Wrangell's, the discount store where they both worked. Yet even with larceny subsidizing them, they couldn't swing an apartment. Every landlord wanted first, last, and deposit, over sixteen hundred dollars. Their car wasn't even worth that much. They scaled down their hopes to a room in a house, but those too were hard to find and, once they did, either the housemates wouldn't take a couple or they asked nearly as much money as the landlords. And Janis had heard a horror story about another Wrangell's employee, three male roommates, and a bong party that had veered out of control.

In the meantime, she and Jimmy worked all day, then ate supper at one of the fast food places in the mall, the day's paper with its useless ads propped between them on a white plastic table. By eight o'clock, they would be bundled back in the tent, freed into sleep. Yet their ease was fleeting. Without fail, they would wake shivering and anxious just after midnight and spend the hours before dawn trapped in a series of restless, fragmented dreams.

"We're homeless, Jimmy," Janis said. "That's what we are, homeless."

"No, we're not," he insisted. "We just haven't found a place we can afford yet."

"We'll be sleeping in our car soon," she moaned.

"Don't be crazy," Jimmy told her, his voice already muffled and distant as he pushed himself back into sleep. He nurtured a recurrent dream in which he carried his blankets alone to a nearby house where he slept finally in comfort, a hand stroking his hair.

Their love life was shot. It was too cold to relinquish layers of clothing now and Janis couldn't hop up and rush to the bathroom when necessary. Besides, neither one felt entirely comfortable making love in the tent anymore. What had once seemed private now seemed remarkably open and on display, despite the growing emptiness of the campground. Deprived, they grew testy with each other. In the ladies' room at work, Janis cried, silently and without warning, overcome by the unexpected comfort of a working hot water tap, the scent of cheap perfume in the air.

Odd Norman, the dwarfish tool department manager, told Jimmy about the farmhouse.

"I'm not sure," he said, in the same quavery voice he used with customers—the voice that told them he was, in fact, completely certain. "I know it's empty, and the old guy's just waiting until the housing development takes off and he can sell it for a bundle. He hasn't lived there in years, you see. Once his wife was gone, he bought a double-wide trailer, stuck it on the far side of his property, and rented out a few fields to neighbors. As far as I know, the house goes empty."

Jimmy called the farmer right away and drove out during his lunch break. The house was even furnished, white sheets over everything. A pleasing smell of musty apples and old wood smoke.

"Go ahead," the farmer said. "Someone should live here, I guess. Everything works, except that old washer downstairs. Even got most of a tank of oil left there in the furnace. I would've drained it, but the trailer's got electric."

< 22 >

He wanted so little for the farmhouse that Jimmy suspected at first Odd Norman had called ahead, offering to subsidize their rent. Nothing down, no damage deposit, no enormous supplement that would ensure the farmer would always receive one last month's rent.

"Forget it," the man waved his hand. His expression soured, and Jimmy worried he'd screwed up, lost this last best chance. But the farmer went on.

"Just don't expect me to come fix anything that breaks on you. I've done my time in that old house. No way I'm going back. Use what you want, treat it like your own, just don't call me."

Jimmy didn't even wait to tell Janis. He raced back to the campsite, broke it down, stuffing tent and sleeping bags into the trunk. After work, he picked up Janis and surprised her, driving west away from the state park. Twenty minutes out of town, but no one wanted to commute even that far. A new subdivision being built a mile or so away already had a ghostly, desperate air to it.

The driveway seemed even longer this time to Jimmy, the lacy weeds higher, the neglected fields a lonesome waving in the fading light. Although it was nearly dusk, they could see the farmhouse from a distance as they approached. Jimmy pointed out the silhouette of the orchard on the hill, the copse of ash and beech trees behind the house, the slanting timbered barn and the ruined stone foundation of another barn the farmer said had burned down a long time ago, when God was a teenager.

Jimmy had a single key, the long skeleton kind that you had to rattle in the lock before it connected.

"Oh, Jimmy," Janis said, as they toured the house. "Oh, Jimmy."

He felt for the first time in a long time as if he had a purpose on earth.

The first thing Janis did was take a bath. The water ran rusty at first, orange-tinged and flecked with oxidized debris from the unused pipes, but Janis wasn't in any particular hurry. By the time the water grew clear and hot, she had swept the blue linoleum tiles, reaching the broom into the corners for what appeared to be leaves, and filled two dustpans. Then she put the stopper in and sat on the closed toilet seat until the tub filled. In the medicine cabinet, she found a pink bottle of bubble bath, the kind used for children's baths. The outside was caked with dusty grime, but the soap still looked fine, a pearly liquid. She poured some in the bath. Their faded blue towels were still damp from the campground. Nothing dried completely out there in the cold. She could smell the moldy undergrowth, the pinched vinegar stink of the camp shower stall, as she dried herself. Tomorrow night, they'd do wash and sleep in scented sheets. Their towels would be warm and thick and sweet-smelling.

Like children in a fairy tale they crept from room to room, pulling dusty sheets from over the furniture, choosing a place to sleep. Four bedrooms in all. Four! Two had single beds.

"The children's rooms," Jimmy said.

The other two featured high double beds, one a sleigh bed, the other with spooled posts at each end.

"Jenny Lind, that's called," Janis said. "I don't know how I know it, but there it is. Look at the bureau, how the legs are spooled, too."

It was that that made them decide the Jenny Lind room was where they'd sleep. They hung their clothes in the closet, smoothing each item, shaking the campground dust away.

"I want to bake muffins on Saturday, and bread, too, maybe," Janis said dreamily as she shed her clothes and climbed naked into the bed. They still slept in their sleeping bags, zipped together to make one cover. Tomorrow evening, they'd scour the closets, begin the cleaning that would make everything theirs.

For the first time in weeks, they made love without anxiety or inhibition. They held nothing back. The old bed creaked from this unfamiliar assault but held steady. Afterwards, the world fell away, and neither one listened for the rustling sound of animal footsteps nor wrestled with needs that could not be met.

In the morning, frost on the field outside. They could feel it even as they lay in bed, an altered light, a blue-tinged chill. Jimmy was the first one up, the first one to climb down the stairs into the living room, brilliant with the dusty white sheets piled beside the red velvet couch. He was the first into the cold sunlit kitchen, the first to see the old refrigerator, a hump-backed, ivory Kelvinator, lying on the floor, its door hanging open and loose, one twisted hinge nearly broken.

More: on the yellow flowered wallpaper behind the kitchen table— a pretty piece of paper Janis had commented upon the previous night, admiring its delicate lines, "Like flowers in an engraving," she said, the color so muted and pleasing—on this admirable wallpaper, a red stain, a jellied clump with painfully bright red rivulets running down into the pale yellow wainscoting.

He would have cleaned it up right then. Quickly, before Janis could see. And right the refrigerator, too. Pretend none of this had happened. The sponge they'd brought with them from the campground had been torn into pieces—yellow fluff scattered on the brown-bricked linoleum. And the refrigerator proved far too heavy for Jimmy alone. And here was Janis in the doorway behind him, dressed in an unfamiliar red plaid robe, one hand holding her throat.

"Who did this?" she said in a whisper. She went to the back door, then the front, all the locks still in place, bolts drawn on the inside. "Check the windows," she said, "go to the basement." He didn't want to, not the basement. Together they put the lights on and walked hand in hand, corner to corner, every window tight even in the basement.

Everything was latched, even painted shut. Dusty rows of preserves still neat on their sway-backed wood shelves. Back in the kitchen, Janis peered at the mess on the wall.

"Jelly," she guessed. Looking closer, yes, raspberry, but not a broken jar in sight, not a single piece of glass.

"The farmer?" she asked Jimmy.

He shook his head. "Why would he rent to us, just to chase us away?"

"Or his children? Does he have children?"

"We didn't hear a thing," Jimmy marveled. "And that"—he pointed to the refrigerator—"must have been incredibly loud. The walls must have shaken."

Janis's face grew hard, thinking of the campground, the frost, winter on its way.

"I'm not leaving," she announced. She filled the kettle and lit the stove defiantly. She pulled plates and cups and saucers from the cupboard, washed them in hot soapy water, and dried them with one of her camp towels. Together, groaning, they lifted the refrigerator back into place and plugged it in.

"We have time for pancakes," she said, digging into their camp cooler. "I'll start them, you get dressed."

He was uncomfortable now, climbing into the shadowed upstairs. Even though he knew no one was there. No one could have been in the kitchen either, but someone had been. He hurried, the air suddenly cooler, and tried not to feel as if he were being watched. When Jimmy came down again, this time clean-shaven, wearing the heavy navy workshirt and tan khakis his work at Wrangell's required, Janis had the coffee poured and was just lifting a pancake onto one of the blue and white farmhouse plates. She'd cleaned the jam off the wall with a faded kitchen towel. He could see the stained towel soaking in pink water in the sink. They ate their pancakes next to the wall. It was marked, but not badly. You had to squint to see it.

He cleaned up while Janis dressed. Most of the yard beyond the kitchen window was overgrown with tall grasses and littered with elongated yellow leaves from a sycamore and tiny brown ones from the yard's other tree, an ancient pear. A few scabby fruits still clung to the highest branches. One corner of the yard, the one beside a slanting shed, was bare rutted dirt. Jimmy could see the remains of more fallen pears there and remembered from his tour with the farmer how the man had clucked at the waste.

"Rats get into these now," he'd said. "And those damn raccoons. Well, let 'em have 'em, I guess. Truth is, I wouldn't eat 'em again. Damn things made me sick. I don't even like 'em canned in sugar syrup."

Jimmy observed other things he missed during that visit: A clothesline dangling from two metal poles, a rusted half of an oil drum lying on its side in what might have once been a garden bed. In the remains of several dahlia plants, black with rot, a broken-handled shovel jammed into the earth.

"You ready?" Janis called. He found her in the front hallway, already wearing her coat and carrying the dirty canvas bag they used for laundry. It wasn't until they had parked the car and were walking into the employee lounge at Wrangell's that Janis unbuttoned her pea coat and Jimmy noticed the blouse she was wearing. A thin flowered blouse with a careful ruffle down the front, shades of red and brown that complemented Janis's hair and deep brown eyes.

"You like it?" she asked, as she pulled on her red and navy Wrangell's smock. "I found it in a drawer, wrapped in tissue." Her voice was stronger than he'd heard it in days, more assured. He just nodded. When he paused outside the restrooms to say goodbye, she kissed him on the mouth, an open lingering kiss that made him pull her

< 27 >

hard to him. She had to push him away to leave the hallway before a supervisor walked by.

"Tonight," she said, "at *home*."

---

That night, they splurged on greasy cheesesteaks in a tavern beside the laundromat. Janis drank two glasses of the house red wine; Jimmy, a half-pitcher of beer. By the time they reached the turnoff for the farmhouse, the tenderness of the night had overtaken them. They leaned against each other all the way up the drive. Jimmy hadn't remembered leaving the porch light on, but it was a welcome surprise. The open door was not. Once again, side by side, they canvassed the house, checking under each bed, in the back of each closet. They rattled the windows, double-checked the locks, and in the end decided that they had not shut the door properly that morning. The house was freezing, but the bed with its clean sheets and thick cocoon of quilts felt wonderful.

In the morning, the kitchen was untouched. Nothing seemed out of place. Janis preened as she cooked bacon, toasted bread. Jimmy simply felt relief. Once again, he washed the dishes while she dressed. Idly, his eyes swept over the yard. He began making plans. A barbecue, new friends from Wrangell's, perhaps a thank-you dinner for Odd Norman. In the spring, they could have a garden. The shed must still house a few tools yet. He remembered the shovel, its broken handle, and looked to the corner where it had been so firmly lodged, but the shovel was no longer there.

Each evening now they sped home, grocery bags in hand. They no longer had to save every penny for the deposits and rent. Janis bought a crock-pot and made beef stew from scratch. She put down a tablecloth, lit the thick white candles she found in a utility closet beside the old mop, the aluminum bucket, the scrubbing brushes. After supper, they

< 28 >

cleaned one room at a time, scrubbing walls and floors. Just like that first morning, Janis gave the orders. Jimmy hadn't known this side of her before, and he marveled at the assured manner in which she claimed the house, room by room. She even went through each closet and drawer, quietly cataloguing their new wealth.

"We have two kids," she told him, after going through the other rooms. "A boy and a girl. Quiet kids, they must be, not a hair out of place. Even their underwear has been ironed."

While they worked inside, the outside seemed to shape up as well. Despite the increasingly dismal mornings, the grayness lifting more reluctantly every day, Jimmy couldn't help but notice how leaves disappeared, how the clothesline was straightened and the metal drum upended and tucked beneath the eaves of the shed. The ground where the shovel had been was cleared and holes dug as if someone had been stopped in the middle of planting bulbs, a task Janis planned to take on once her day off arrived. One morning, he saw a figure moving around the ruins of the barn. A woman, he could tell that much. She turned to face him, and he caught the briefest glimpse of a pale face. By the time he thrust his feet into his boots and opened the back door, she was gone. Although he stalked the grass nearly all the way up to the woods looking for her, she had utterly vanished. He did not mention any of this to Janis, afraid to disturb her new joy, but he brought a new lock home from work and replaced the old skeleton keys with standard keys he cut himself at Wrangell's. Janis laughed at him, calling him house-proud, and that was fine with him, as long as she was happy. And she was. Blindly, ridiculously happy. When one morning, she herself noticed a change—a row of bedsheets, glowing white on the clothesline—she assumed he'd repaired the old washer. How, he marveled inwardly, could she be so dense, knowing they spent every free moment together? Still, he kept the truth from her.

On the night before their first day off, it hailed so hard all the windows shook. Janis, waking, thought for a moment they were back in the campground.

"Oh my god," she said aloud, her eyes still pinched shut.

The corners of the tent were always wet from dew. She'd learned to keep any extra clothes in the car and place her shoes in a plastic bag each night. Still, the edges of the sleeping bag inevitably soaked up the dampness from the tent walls. And when it rained, no matter how well they'd positioned the old tarps above and beneath them, they ended up completely wet and shivering. She almost cried when she opened her eyes and began to make out the solid, dry contours of the room.

"Oh my god," she whispered again, this time in gratitude.

*Safe.* They must have had the thought at the same time, warm under the covers, burrowing close to one another, when they heard the front door open, the squeak of its hinges like a single high-pitched whistle.

They waited for footsteps on the stairs, and when those didn't come, both Janis and Jimmy jumped out of bed and began hurriedly dressing.

---

The woman Jimmy had seen by the barn ruins was seated in the living room on the figured red velvet couch that Janis admired so much. She had nothing with her, not a purse or a suitcase. Her red-knuckled hands, noticeably big and broad for a woman, were empty, loosely clasped in front of her. A woman, in her early forties perhaps, with brown hair going to gray, cut in a peculiar style—clipped severely in front, left much longer in the back. She wore a pair of plain navy blue polyester trousers, a pink cotton blouse, and a long gray cardigan that might have once belonged to a man, all of it clean and pressed and dry. She did not smile at Janis or Jimmy, nor did she seem surprised

< 30 >

to see them. Her eyes were flat, her skin pale and chapped, her lips one rigid line.

"You're finally up," she said. "It's time we met."

She said her name was Peabody. Marian Peabody, the farmer's wife.

Jimmy was glad Janis was in her own jeans and turtleneck for a change. He began to introduce himself and Janis, but Janis interrupted.

"You can't just walk in here, you know," she said, tilting her chin. "We pay rent."

Marian Peabody shrugged her off. "A tiny, inadequate sum, I'm sure."

"He didn't ask for more."

"*He*," and here the woman's voice resembled a heel grinding hard at the earth, "*he* has no rights here anymore."

"It's his house, he says."

She looked as if she would spit. Instead, the words ratcheted out: She had been away. Despite her absence, this was still her house. No one could take that from her.

"We're not leaving," Janis said. "Get used to that, Mrs. Peabody. We're paid up and we're not going anywhere."

---

Jimmy tried to find the farmer's telephone number, but the slip on which Odd Norman had written it had long been lost and the phone company had no listing for the name Jimmy wrote on the rent check. He drove to the mailbox where he met the farmer that first time, turned up the rutted gravel drive, and drove almost a quarter mile into a logged hillside until the driveway ended at a turquoise mobile home. Every shade was drawn, but he could hear a television or radio playing as he knocked on the door, and the farmer promptly answered, looking sleepy and disheveled.

"So she's come to you, has she?" he said. "Like I said, you keep me out of this. You want to pay me less rent, you go ahead. I'm not coming to collect. I'd as soon see the place disappear than fight for it. Been away, is that what she tells you? She says the farm is hers, does she? Ask her who's still paying the tax on it? Ask her...no, better yet, clear out while you can."

"Clear out? We just moved in!"

"You want to take your chances, you go right ahead. But I'll tell you this, she tried to have me killed is what she did. Talked to buddies of mine, guys I was in the army with, for crissakes. They thought she was joking. Snickered behind my back, saying that's what you get when you marry a girl half your age—a kid playing tricks on you. As if Marian ever messed around in her life. But when my vision started doubling, and my gut pains wouldn't quit, my buddies told me what I should've already known. 'She's poisoning you,' they said. That no one ever proved, but all my ailments magically disappeared now, didn't they, once the sheriff collected her. 'Have a little drink with me, Clyde,' she'd say. Ha! The kids, they were on her side, wailing like crazy. No one could expect me to live with that, not feeling the way I did. I gave them a call, that agency, the kiddie protection league, and they swooped down and took them away, kicking and caterwauling. Temporarily, you understand. I'd already moved into town on the advice of my lawyer, went to sleeping at the Crest City motel. The gal in the office was an old friend of mine. She cut the rate a little for me.

"The kids? The kids?" The farmer sucked at his cheeks. "Well, when they gave 'em back, I sent the girl off to my aunt's upstate. They couldn't take the boy in, not after what he did, trying to come after me like that. The kiddie police came back again, and I said, take 'im, I'm not looking out for my back every minute. No one could expect me to, could they? Ten years old, big man, tried to brain me with a shovel while I'm dozing on the couch. Because of what I did to his mother, he says. What I did! Wasn't she the one with all the problems? Drinking her liquor from a jelly glass? 'Go to a doctor,' I said, 'get yourself cured.'

"You know what she told me?" He squinted as if he could still hardly believe his ears. "She said, 'You'll pay for this.' And here I was offering help. I didn't even say a word when I found out they'd let her off and she'd run away, picking up the kids as she went. I could've divorced her ass good, and she wouldn't have gotten a cent that way, either, not a penny. I wouldn't have let her take the goddamn kids like that, not without a word. I did still have some damn rights and she knew it."

"Kids?" Jimmy gulped, imagining a whole family now, crowding into the rooms he and Janis had claimed. "She doesn't have any kids with her."

"No, she wouldn't, would she," the farmer spat. He whistled for his dogs, two old hounds who galloped out of nowhere to bark and snarl at Jimmy.

"Word to the wise," he told Jimmy with a mean smile, "get yourself a big ol' dog. She hates 'em. You get a good, fierce one he'll chase her right into the night, and you can just lock up tight behind her, listen to the wind come up, and know it's only taking her farther away, like a little bit of trash dumped on the property line."

———————

He was beyond despair. He couldn't imagine where they'd go. They'd spent a lot of their savings on a new television, too expensive even with their Wrangell's discount. There was a shelter in Roselin, the next town over. Janis would die. No, they'd sell the car first, get new jobs, walk to work. His chest contracted. He could hardly get a breath. "Oh baby," he whispered, "oh, Janis baby, I'm so sorry."

But when he arrived back at the farmhouse, Janis didn't even grill

< 33 >

him about the farmer's response. She and Mrs. Peabody were in the kitchen, drinking coffee from pink-flowered cups.

"Marian's going to stay," she told Jimmy, "and we are too."

Seated at the kitchen table, Marian spoke as if her words were rehearsed: "I don't drive. It might be useful to me, after all, if you two would stay." Her speech included them both, but it was to Janis she directed her words. In fact, it seemed to Jimmy that she avoided even glancing in his direction.

Despite their newfound camaraderie, Janis was nothing but direct: "You've got that right, Marian. We're staying as long as we like, as long as we pay rent."

The rain, memories of the campground spurred her on. *Just try and evict us,* Jimmy heard beneath her words. *Just try.*

Later, as they drove to town alone, she told him that Marian had no place else to go. If she couldn't stay here, she'd have to sleep in the fields. "She'd be homeless, Jimmy," Janis declared. Her family wouldn't talk to her after she left her husband. No one around here would give her a job. Her husband, the farmer, never sent her a dime. She had nothing, nothing to live on. But, of course, she owned a house—their house. Jimmy didn't even think to mention the kids. The farmer had lied about so much; he'd probably made up the story about the kids, too, right there on the spot, one more reason for Jimmy to drive away Marian.

———

At first, sharing was not a hardship, and on the surface, their lives went on normally. Jimmy and Janis rattled down the driveway in the bluish haze of morning and returned to a dim yellow light in an upstairs window. Marian had claimed one of the front rooms with a single bed in it and the door was always shut and—Janis checked—locked. Sometimes, as they entered the house, they heard the indis-

< 34 >

tinct melodies of a transistor radio; other times, Marian's own voice, an even incantation that went on for hours.

"Praying," Jimmy guessed.

"For us to leave," Janis smirked. "Fat chance."

On their days off, they plunged into home improvement, sanding and refinishing old floorboards, nailing down curling linoleum, waxing, polishing. Janis continued to claim the house, room by room, drawer by drawer, and Marian, for all her initial possessiveness, did not seem to notice, let alone care. They picked up items from the drugstore for her when she asked: aspirin, baby powder, a metal canister of adhesive bandages, a pair of hair-cutting scissors she used to give herself a new, softer haircut that compelled Jimmy and Janis to reassess her age. She might not be all that much older than they were, they reckoned. This awareness made them both a little uncomfortable, as if they couldn't trust their own eyes, as if she'd lost years in the brief time she'd spent with them. Occasionally, she requested something from a specialty shop: a bottle of sherry, a ball of rose tweed wool, black shoe polish. She didn't seem to possess a single cent. At least she never offered to pay for anything. Janis, toting up their expenses, quietly suggested to Jimmy that they stop paying the farmer rent since he apparently had decided to forego his own responsibility. Jimmy thought she meant they should pay Marian.

"What," Janis said, "are you kidding? When she's living here with us and eating our food?"

A whole month went by, then another—rain and sleet, the first whispers of snow—and no one arrived to protest the missing rent. Under the unexpected weight of an ice storm, limbs from the pear tree cracked and fell, and someone—Marian apparently—dragged the branches behind the shed and sawed them into firewood.

Marian didn't seem to mind the cold. In fact, her interest clearly lay outside. From the kitchen window, Jimmy saw her emerge from the old barn, empty except for a few rusty kids' bicycles and a broken wagon. He tracked her from the window as she wandered through the stubbled icy field, wearing her usual outfit, topped only by that thin gray sweater. As he spied from the window, Marian gazed intently toward the woods and raised a hand as if she were greeting someone. But when he looked with her, the woods were still and empty, and the sky remained the dull charcoal of a winter dusk, patches of snow sunk in the ditch by the driveway. He could hear Janis in the upstairs hall, cranking up the thermostat, and he shivered as he thought of Marian in her ragged sweater. For the first time, he rummaged in the back of the hall closet, emerging with a heavy wool jacket, brown plaid. A young man's jacket, the pockets heavy with forgotten treasures: a smooth green stone, bottlecaps, loose pieces of tobacco. Coatless himself, he carried the jacket out into the dim field, turning in circles as he looked for Marian, who was suddenly there, right beside him.

"You'll catch your death," Jimmy said, shocked as much by the chiding tone in his own voice as by the delicate feel of the woman's shoulders when he draped the jacket around her, the surprising pure blue of her eyes.

"Well, hello, Jimmy," she said, as if she'd just noticed his existence.

After that, the brown plaid jacket took up residence on the coat rack by the kitchen door, its absence signaling Marian's as well, and Jimmy found himself continually checking the hooks, then scanning the white fields below the purple sky, sighting her the way another man might look out for deer out of season: starved and feeble and ready.

---

She was the easiest of housemates, a mere cipher on the edge of their own existence, and yet it wasn't long before a battle began. Every day,

< 36 >

a new insult, a fresh intrusion arrived to irritate Janis: Marian left dishes in the sink. Janis washed a dish if she liked the pattern. Otherwise, she plucked it from the sink and deposited it into the garbage. Mouse droppings were discovered in the cupboards. Janis set traps between the saucepans, baited with peanut butter; Marian scattered breadcrumbs in their bedroom closet. Jimmy found himself standing inside the open closet door, breathing in the comforting aroma of freshly baked bread. He had to force himself to whisk up the crumbs before Janis discovered them.

Then came the cough. Marian developed an insistent, baneful bark that could not be calmed by Janis's offers of tea or lozenges or a good thwack on the back.

"See a doctor," Janis told her. "We'll drive you."

"Oh, listen to her," Janis told him. "Could a cough be more fake?"

There were times when Jimmy longed for a straight haunting like their first night. Plates crashing against the walls in the night. Furniture moving. All of it unexplained. The reality of Marian worried him far more than any ghost could have. The way she never got angry at Janis, just stared at her blankly, like one of those old ladies at the nursing home where his grandmother had served out her last blind, baffled days. The way she stalked the periphery of the old barn ruins, her head bobbing up and down as if she were in conversation. The way her fingers brushed lightly against his own when they passed plates at the table, causing a confusing heat to swirl deep in his belly.

And there were other times, when he held Janis in his arms and felt the thin blades of Marian's shoulder; when Janis—wearing her pilfered blouse—swept into the Wrangell's employee lounge and the fierce, musty scent of Marian filled the air between them; when, woolgathering at the kitchen window, he thought he heard the whisper of his name and lumbered toward the back door to find Marian already

< 37 >

at the stoop, one reddened hand reaching for the metal doorknob. At those moments, he felt as if he recognized her, and he was glad she was near.

Despite Janis's skepticism, he believed in Marian. She had lost weight, revealing a fragility that pierced Jimmy, that made him want to gather her up and tend to her. But when Jimmy grew awkward making love with Marian just down the hall (her coughing made her present in a way she hadn't been before), Janis grew angry. "Don't you let her stop us," she whispered in his ear. Marian's presence did nothing to deter Janis, who hollered and moaned and beat at the bed beside Jimmy with a roaring intensity he'd never seen in her and which frightened him.

"It's our house," she told Jimmy in a voice that no longer whispered. "We can do whatever the hell we please here." Neither of them said a word when moments later doors began slamming all over the house, a grander version of Marian's cough.

---

One evening, when Janis was unexpectedly stuck with an overtime shift, Jimmy drove home alone to pick up their laundry. He figured he'd surprise Janis when he picked her up with folded piles of clean towels and blue jeans. As usual, the house appeared blank and deserted, save for the light in Marian's window. As he crept along the upstairs hall, trying to be quiet, he was surprised to see her bedroom door open. He could hear her struggling to suppress that itchy cough she couldn't seem to shake, and thought, too, he heard her call to him as he passed.

In the dim golden light of her bedside lamp, he could barely make out Marian's figure, sitting on the edge of the bed, her back to the door. An overwhelmingly pungent scent (mint? camphor?) nearly caused him to stumble as he crossed the threshold. At the sound, Marian

< 38 >

pulled back, and the light her body had blocked spilled over her. He could see now that her back and shoulders were bare. She held the edge of the bedsheet against the front of her body. Beside her on the bed was a jar of eucalyptus liniment Janis had bought for her own sore muscles when they were still sleeping in the campground.

"I'm sorry," Jimmy stuttered. "I thought you . . ."

"Come here a moment, Jim," Marian said, keeping her face away from him.

There was a spot just below her shoulder blades, behind her rib cage, she said. She could feel a tightness there, but couldn't reach it with the liniment.

"If you wouldn't mind," she said, holding the jar out to him.

His weight sagged the mattress and caused Marian to tip in his direction. In the warm pooled light, her skin was near golden, as grainy and perfect as an old photograph. The cold liniment burned on his fingertips when he rubbed it lightly in the center of her back. Although he'd been dead tired as he drove home from Wrangell's, he felt brilliantly awake now, focused on his task. Marian tipped her head forward, exposing the long line of her bare back. He kneaded a muscled knot beneath her shoulder blade, and she groaned softly, a deeply pleasurable human sound that caused a hot ache to swell again within Jimmy. He could feel himself responding and was about to pull away when Marian suddenly turned to thank him, his busy hand swept across her breasts, and he felt her nipples rise beneath the palm of his hand. For a second, they were both stunned, but she didn't move, not even as Jimmy began—his fingers still slick with liniment—to circle her breasts. By the time she lay back on the bed, his eyes were half-closed, his lips were stroking her left nipple, and his hand was moving down her stomach. Her body rippled, actually rippled, and this thrilled him as if he'd just made her come alive beneath him. Before long, it was Jim crying out. He heard his voice as if it were calling him from another room—agonized, ecstatic. Only when he was flinging his old car down the black country road, racing to reach Wrangell's before Janis's shift ended, his entire body still charged with the encounter, did he begin to realize what he'd done. Then Marian's parting words—*This is between us*—seemed less an absolution, less even a colluding promise, than a shadowy, ever-lasting alliance. And, indeed, when an exhausted Janis moved into his sleeping arms later that night, he saw that Marian had taken up residence between them, her solemn blue gaze both urging him on and holding him back.

------

The next day, Janis's shift was once again extended three hours. A Wrangell's trick, this "temporary shift extension." Until the holidays were over, she said during their break, she'd be on overtime, without the extra pay.

"No big deal. I can use whatever money I can get," she told Jimmy, who noticed that she said "I" not "We."

Since Marian had moved in and they'd stopped paying rent, they'd banked most of the money they'd been paying Peabody, but Janis was losing her fear of falling off the edge. Marian's abandoned wardrobe, once a boon, didn't thrill Janis any longer. Jimmy was sorry to see her discard her old clothes from the campground, sorry too when she put away the simple belted housedresses and the delicate floral blouses. He'd grown used to them, even found them sexy in a way the tight sweaters and low-slung jeans Janis now bought from Wrangell's never could be. There were other things she desired: tall leatherette boots, eye makeup, a shearling jacket. No, she wouldn't complain about the extra work. Her discount would be bumped up five percent with the additional hours.

At first, Jimmy would hang around town for the few hours after work, just as he and Janis had done while they were at the campground. He'd take himself out to a hamburger dinner, go to a movie, or roam the mall. Janis groused at the money he was spending. Why, for instance, should he buy restaurant food when the refrigerator and freezer were both packed from her weekly excursions to Wrangell's new food mart? Janis instructed him in the crock-pot's finer points, left him with a fistful of recipe cards, and all but ordered him to stay home each evening.

Yet it was Marian who began to cook. Blue willow china platters that had somehow escaped Janis's plundering appeared on the table laden with fried chicken and biscuits, green beans cooked in bacon fat, a meatloaf not unlike his mother's. He ate with abandon, barely suppressing a hum of pleasure that arose without warning. She watched him, hardly touching the food herself. In fact, she'd grown so thin, now it was Marian who filched Janis's clothes. Afterwards, washing dishes together, his hands would slip again, rubbing against Janis's old blue sweater, unbuttoning jeans as familiar as his own, and before he could catch his breath, they would be back in her golden room and he would be in her, his heart about to burst.

*Remember this*, Marian commanded, *remember this*.

The truth was she made him forget. Each night he struggled to wake and push himself down the stairs and back into the car. Twice he was late getting back to Wrangell's, and the parking lot was nearly empty, except for the night crew and an idiot stock clerk, who clearly had a crush on Janis. Wally, red-headed Wally, Wally the weight-lifting gossip, who wandered from department to department with his price gun and cart, spreading rumors of his own devising.

"The car wouldn't start," he explained to Janis the last time, while Wally smirked in the background.

"You leave me waiting like that one more time and I might just take that boy up on his offer of a ride," Janis said as she closed the car door.

< 41 >

"I'll clean the plugs," he promised.

"You do that," she said. After a pause in which they drove through downtown and turned onto the black country road: "Hey, I heard something about our Marian today."

Jimmy's groin still tingled. His head was full of images of Marian, naked on her stomach as he approached the bed, and he was grateful the dark hid his tangled hair, his own swollen lips.

"Oh, yeah?"

"The kids the farmer mentioned. They're real, all right, and they aren't farmed out," Janis informed him. "Wally told me. They're both dead. A car accident. Our Marian was drinking, he said. Three teenagers from Meredith died as well. They were in the other car. That's why she's been away, you see. She must have been in jail! All those dead kids. And that's why she doesn't drive. God, it all adds up, doesn't it?"

She fingered a hand-knitted red scarf she'd taken from a hidden cedar chest in the girl's room, loosening its knot around her throat so that a gash of her own white skin appeared between the folds and glowed in the dark car.

"*Wally,*" Jimmy spat.

"Not just Wally. Claudia in Housewares told me the same story. Her nephew was in Scouts with Marian's boy. But here's something funny: Wally swears Marian poisoned herself before the trial—with arsenic the farmer kept in the old barn."

"What an ass." Jimmy's hands shook on the steering wheel.

"Wally says she smuggled it into her food. He says it took her days to die."

"He mixed up Peabody's story, didn't he?"

"Obviously, but *Wally*..."

"Mention his name one more time, and I'll drive off the road," Jimmy declared.

"Well, what's wrong with *you?*"

That night for the first time, Jimmy slept downstairs alone, his heart thrumming with the loss Janis had tried to hand him.

———————

She exhausted him. She revived him. She slayed him. She brought him to life. At work, he was clumsy, a dumb smile plastered on his face, the kind of smile that Janis once said made him look like a cat with buttered whiskers. He drifted off in conversations, licking his butter, the almost physical memory of her touch.

"Someone's getting some," Donny from Outdoors/Recreation remarked as he passed through Hardware and Tools and caught Jimmy, blissfully open-mouthed before a rack of plastic elbow pipes. Odd Norman, who'd been quietly directing Wally in the next aisle, overheard and poked his head around the corner. Donny immediately moved on, a curious Wally scuttling in his wake.

Odd Norman was his supervisor and the closest Jimmy had to a male friend. Normally, Jimmy would have shared any news in his life with him, but the situation with Marian was too odd. No one knew they shared a house with her. How could he tell Odd Norman about his new home life? And yet, like any besotted lover, Jimmy's whole being sang with the desire to hear her name, to casually throw out, *Marian says... Marian told me... Marian, Marian, Marian.* But, of course, he couldn't. He couldn't. Could he?

"Marian Peabody, you say?" Odd Norman glanced at him sharply, the dimpled lines in his long handsome face emphasized by his concern. "I knew her as a girl. Quiet kid, a real sweetheart, the kind of kid who brought frosted cupcakes to school on other people's birthdays. She deserved better. She would have been the best of wives to the right man, you know, a real homemaker."

Jimmy grinned and nodded. He began to explain their situation, Janis—he emphasized it was Janis—inviting Marian to live with them.

He flushed red, but he couldn't stop himself, he had to share: *One night*, he began, *when Janis was at work…*

A customer wandered up the aisle, talking, as customers usually did, over Odd Norman's head to Jimmy, who immediately deferred the man's question. Odd Norman pursed his lips as he led the man away toward the socket wrenches. Only much later, as Jimmy was clocking out, did Odd Norman catch up to him again, tapping Jimmy on the hip.

"Not Marian Peabody?" Odd Norman told him. "Jim, you must be wrong about that."

"She has such pretty eyes," he told Odd Norman, "you'd never guess it."

"Can I come see her?" his boss asked.

"Sure," Jimmy said. He didn't want Odd Norman at the farmhouse, didn't want him to see Marian, most of all, he didn't want to lose his evening alone with her.

"How about Thursday?" Thursday was Janis's day off.

"Tonight, Jim," he said. "I'd like to come tonight."

"Oh, sure," Jimmy said, fuming. "Any time."

They were still at the table when Odd Norman drove up in his ticking Volkswagen, Jimmy savoring a wedge of warm pear pie. She heard Odd Norman long before he did, and by the time headlights swept across the front porch, she had fled upstairs. Jimmy could hear her door close, the lock snapping into place. He had to smile. If she wasn't around, Odd Norman wouldn't stay long. But Odd Norman wouldn't take any of Jimmy's excuses. He reached for the banister and mounted the stairs, turning unerringly toward Marian's room when he reached the landing.

"Marian?" he called as he knocked on the door. "It's Norm Kesky. Open the door. Marian, you remember me, don't you? Honey, I want to talk to you."

< 44 >

To Jimmy's great surprise, the door swung open.

Odd Norman took a step back. He gazed upwards. A range of expressions crossed his face: joy, awe, sorrow. "Oh, Marian," he murmured, "it *is* you."

From where he stood, Jimmy couldn't see Marian at all. Norman had one of Marian's hands in his own, and because she was so much taller, the little manager appeared to be on his knees, his face upturned, shining.

"You know you can't stay, don't you, sweetheart? You know this isn't your home anymore."

"You don't think I deserve this," she said.

"It's not yours," Norman said, gently. He nodded toward Jimmy. "*He's* not yours. They're gone, Marian. It's over now."

A series of crashes began as if every ordinary article Marian had collected during her stay—the Band-Aid tin, a black pot of shoe polish, a drinking glass emblazoned with a beer logo—was being hurled at the walls.

"You have to go, Marian. Leave."

"Hey," Jimmy objected, but no one seemed to hear him.

A rhythmic shushing sound began as Norman spoke: *Huhnuna, huhnuna, huhnuna.* Jimmy did not recognize it as weeping until Norman kissed her hand and said goodbye, leading Jimmy down the stairs and out the front door with him. He'd never even removed his coat or the peaked blue hat he wore.

"Jim—" he began.

"What the hell do you think you're doing, Norman?" Jimmy demanded, but he didn't wait for an answer. He slammed the car door Norman held open and stood there, his arms folded across his chest, until Norman shook his head and finally started his car.

She wasn't in her room when he returned. Not in the bathroom, the kitchen, the living room. He searched the house in a fever, calling her name. He thought about calling for his dogs, dogs he didn't own, great black hounds with red-rimmed jaws and wild eyes who would run through the house, a mad gallop that would shake the walls and unfasten the doors from their hinges and chase Marian back into his arms. The brown plaid jacket was missing from the hook, and so he raced outside again, coatless himself. Beside the house the barren woods rustled, a brittle rattle that he mistook for her footsteps. He bellowed, but the wind snatched her name the moment it left his mouth. Hours it seemed he searched for her, inside and out, his hands numb with cold, the old batteries in his flashlight giving way while he was high up in the frost-slick fields. The wind died down, the night became unbearably still, and he was nearly lost when far away, another car door slammed, and Jimmy peered from the hilltop to see taillights retreating down the long driveway. He stumbled toward them, sliding, losing his balance, falling hard again and again until he knelt trembling by the barn ruins, his legs too weak to move. He could see lamps springing on, Janis claiming the house, each uncurtained window framing her escalating emotions. Desperate, he called out to her, but the black night had become her mirror and she was blind to him.

< 46 >

# MY SISTERS

My sisters began dying in earnest the year I turned five. Eve was nine; Marie, eleven: two skinny brown-haired girls with skin so pale that, before the diagnoses, neighbors nearly believed our parents might be starving them, a parenting trend that year. It actually took a while to dissuade the law and relatives like my Aunt Olivia that this was not the case. One day in late September, Eve collapsed during school recess. She had been skipping rope with Marie and the Sheba sisters and our neighbor, tiny, tomboy Ginny Minster, who could walk on her hands. They were playing double-dutch, the Sheba sisters turning the ropes, while a half-dozen girls surrounded them and sang:

Mother, Mother, I am ill
Call for the doctor over the hill.
In came the doctor,
In came the nurse,
In came the lady with the alligator purse.
Measles, said the doctor.
Mumps, said the nurse.
Dead, said the lady with the alligator purse.
Out goes the doctor,
Out goes the nurse,
Out goes the lady with the alligator purse.

Ginny insisted upon being the doctor; Marie was the nurse; Eve, tall and regal for her age, was the lady with the alligator purse. Their entries into the spinning ropes were on cue and faultless. Then it came time to exit. *Out goes the doctor*, and Ginny flew away; *Out*

< 47 >

*goes the nurse*, and Marie skipped easily back into the crowd; *Out goes the lady*... and precisely at the moment she was to exit, Eve simply wilted, sinking onto the pavement, tangled in jump rope, the song dying around her.

*Light bulb*, Eve mumbled later, meaning, we gradually discovered, that she felt like a light bulb. Click, and the world went black; click, and she was in an ambulance; click, and she was awake again, IVs in her arm, a plastic oxygen tube tickling each nostril. She swatted the air around her as if warning us all away from her switch, the one she believed someone was messing with.

But within a month, Eve was out of the hospital, on a regular schedule of transfusions, and well again, it seemed. Kind of. Our family had almost taken her illness in stride, my father jotting Eve's appointment dates on the calendar beside my Pee-Wee football games and Marie's piano lessons, as if she'd taken up a new hobby.

Then Marie fell off the city bus.

Like Eve, she'd been fine a moment before. She'd been standing with the Sheba sisters at the front of the bus, which was nearing their corner. The bus cranked and wheezed to its stop, and as the Sheba sisters climbed off, Marie fell after them, headlong like a logged tree, down the metal bus steps straight onto the curb. The Sheba sisters, still undone from those moments on the playground when Eve could not be called back to consciousness, began wailing straightaway, and the bus driver scooped up an unconscious Marie and drove ten blocks to the hospital, squeezing the bus into the Emergency entryway to the thunderous applause of the other passengers.

Like Eve, Marie, with her narrow face battered from the fall, spent days in the hospital, although, unlike with Eve, the process of deducing the cause of her mysterious collapse was considerably shortened. Just for good measure, they hauled me in and I spent a few days having tests too before they determined I did not inherit that rare congenital blood disorder my sisters shared, the way they shared a bedroom and sweaters and a thousand plastic barrettes. The only boy, I'd always had my own room, my own toys, and now my own promise of a long, lonelier life. Marie saw my dismay and knew it immediately for what it was.

"Don't worry, Arthur," she said. "One of us will shoot you when we're croaking."

She was still at home then, dragging from room to room in Eve's new pink plaid pajamas, but she weakly pretended to draw a pair of pistols from an invisible holster, twirl them in the air, and blow me away.

From then on, all of us—Eve, Marie, and me and Don and Evelyn, our parents—began to look at everything with a new wariness. It took so little, we were realizing, to become separated from this world. And we weren't alone. With this new understanding, we gained entry into a world of like-minded folk, people who knew with real certainty that the world we knew and had taken for granted might disappear any moment.

As, of course, it did.

———————

Olivia, my mother's sister, kidnapped me after the girls died. Matter-of-factly. With aplomb. She lured me to her kitchen with a fresh-baked pie, an intoxication of cream and chocolate and a crunchy, sugary caramel bathed in what I'd later learned was whiskey and ground Ambien. I slept while she half-carried, half-walked me to the back seat of her car. Slept through two states and woke groggy to a cold Coke on ice. *Light bulb.* Drugged again, I slept until finally the sun broke and I was in a frame house in the country, wearing a cowboy shirt, jeans, and a lariat tie. *Light bulb.* A voice I almost recognized was calling me to supper.

"Come on, now, Arthur," Olivia called. "Your daddy's home."

A stranger, of course, smiling shyly, bemused and ready to play the game from the head of the table. What could I say? When weeks later, finally, my parents found me, I greeted them not with relief but with surprise, because I'd been sure that I'd died too and now I was in my aunt's dark heaven, pie and whiskey on the table, waiting for the girls to come home.

< 50 >

# PEARL DIVING

The winter my father disgraced us, my mother told us her version of a children's story—Henny Penny without the relieving idiocy. We had been trapped inside all day while outside a snowstorm consumed every familiar landmark, and when finally we arrived at dinner time, we ate the meal—thinly sliced beef and buttered new potatoes, a tiny, bitter endive salad—in almost utter silence, as if the snow had muffled our conversation as well. Afterwards my father disappeared without a word into the den, and my mother rinsed the dishes. Then she poured herself another tumbler of vermouth, lit a cigarette, and otherwise prepared herself to amuse my brother Henry and me with games of Scrabble and blind man's canasta...and, as the evening wore on, her own renditions of well-known fairy tales, tales that centered on the town of Clementsville where my parents lived.

We were far too old for such evenings. I was fifteen and Henry seventeen, but even if the storm had not held us captive we had nothing better to do. We never stayed in Clementsville long enough to make a single friend. This was our first trip back from the Holt School in over six months, and the atmosphere was tense, although we didn't yet know why. While my mother straightened the kitchen, we smoked a joint in Henry's room before reappearing, dutifully stoned and greedy for the bowls of butterscotch pudding that in the past accompanied my mother's twisted fairy tales.

In my mother's version of Henny Penny, the sky really does fall, no joke. "First come the clouds," she said, holding out a hand to pan-

< 51 >

tomime catching bits of cloud that transformed quickly from damp, full-bodied orbs into sweet-smelling mist.

"Close your eyes, boys," she told us.

At her command, we offered our palms, which she dusted with a feathery tissue. Once the clouds drifted loose, she went on, the sky rearranged itself, blue washing into blue, before it too began to let go, thin chips of varying hues—azure, sapphire, cerulean, robin's egg—coating roofs and streets.

"Bits of fallen sky caught in the fur of animals," she said, "they flickered on eyelashes. Cold beyond cold, those chips were. When one fell upon your bare skin, you jumped as if you had been burned." To illustrate, my mother touched our cheeks with a piece of ice from her glass of vermouth.

The world grew dim as colors faded. Chalk-gray trees, iron grass. Another set of clouds, previously hidden, descended. These were dirty and ragged in comparison to those that came before, like ratty tumble-weeds. "You couldn't resist kicking one," she said, "and watching it bounce above the huge spread oak and into the town pond beyond, engulfing the nasty-tempered swans. No one seemed to notice the spiraling tunnel forming above, a shadowed hole that swelled in size until, like a giant vacuum, it began sweeping people toward heaven. One by one at first, then batches, whole swarms writhing upwards. Soon nearly everyone in town was beating the flat, chill air, holding arms aloft like Superman."

"Then what?" Henry and I begged. We were stoned enough that our own arms were half-rising in response, our feet twitching involuntarily as if we, too, were beginning the long journey from the bottom of the world.

My father poked in his head, drawn by the irresistible rasping of my mother's whispering voice. We ignored him; he hadn't felt cloud on his palm or sky on his cheek.

< 52 >

"Elaine," he began, frowning as he grasped the elements of her tale.

"Don't start, Jay," my mother responded. "It's my story this time." She looked straight at him, her drink tinkling in her hand. "I think I'm owed a few of my own, don't you?"

---

Everyone in our family told stories. We relayed them as a matter of course: simple lies, long, complicated misdirections. Throughout the fall, Henry had labored over his college application essays, fabricating autobiographies, each one more fantastic, more heroic, than the last.

"What do you mean, 'aviator'?" I asked, looking over his shoulder. "You don't fly planes."

"I could," said Henry.

"But you don't. And you don't do humanitarian runs to . . . *the Maldives?* Henry, no one is going to believe this crap." In response, my brother had offered a series of dismissive gestures that let me know that any attempts to shame him would go unheeded.

That winter evening when my mother challenged him, my father imitated Henry's quick twist of the mouth, his left eyebrow slightly raised and held, the shoulder shrug. An insult acknowledged, but not owned.

*Go ahead*, he seemed to say, *tell your story. But you have no idea how a tale truly grows smooth and fulsome, how a story becomes a life.*

And the next morning, my mother did relate another tale, this one rife with accusations and dismay.

"If only," she pronounced at the end, "he'd stolen enough so that we could disappear."

She said this, not to us, but over the phone to her long-estranged sister Ginny. Henry and I did not know Ginny, who until recently had lived in Europe. My aunt had married a far richer man than my father, although one with a more humble pedigree. He, too, had recently tumbled from grace—only my Uncle Jack's lapse involved a woman, and my aunt, I understood from eavesdropping, stood to gain rather than lose from his indiscretion, especially as long as she retained custody of her daughter, my cousin, Laura.

Of Laura I knew very little. She was almost exactly my age, our birthdays two days apart, and, like us, she'd been sent off to school at an early age, inaugurating her own troubled history. The exact nature of Laura's indiscretions was not clear, but I knew she had attended no fewer than seven schools in nine years. Even as my mother and Ginny considered their own options, the subject of Laura and her latest debacle hovered close to the forefront of their discussion. As they talked, my mother nipped at a set of needlepoint cushion covers with a pair of manicure scissors. The needlepoint design incorporated my father's initials, and the scissors made tiny kissing noises as she snipped, leaving shreds of blue thread on the rug around her feet.

Toward what should have been the end of our extended weekend at home, my mother finally told us what we already knew: our father had been caught in one of his stories. And yet, remarkably, he had not been fired. His position had been altered, responsibilities lightened and so forth, and he was required to undergo a course of therapy with a Dr. Alice Chase. More to the point, he was bound to make complete restitution for certain missing items, which he swore he had merely misplaced. This final stipulation would require, we learned, severe family sacrifices.

"We can keep the house," my mother said, "but we'll have to let other things go—at least until we get on our feet again."

It took us a minute to understand the portent of her statement. Hearing our mother's edict, Henry, normally placid and easy-going, began to rage, and when that failed, he wheedled and schemed. Our mother remained adamant.

"We have no choices here," she said, flexing her tiny scissors.

We had no way of knowing whether she was lying.

That day, the weather warmed dramatically, and rain arrived, beating the snow into swift, slushy streams that roared through the dirty gutters of Clementsville. All the pure beauty disappeared, and the town emerged, mud-streaked and tattered. Our mother drove us to the Holt campus, two hours away, where, high on white crosses, Henry and I cleaned out our dorm rooms in a haphazard frenzy, hurling half-sealed boxes into the back of her Audi wagon. Our mother said little to us, but on the way home she swerved into the parking lot of Clementsville High School. Twenty minutes later, just as our hearts were pattering down to normal speed, we were enrolled in the yellow-bricked public school of our hometown.

"This isn't real," Henry said once we were back in the car, our new schedules in hand. "This isn't happening."

"Pretend, then," my mother said, without a trace of meanness. "Just pretend that it is."

Instead of calming Henry down, my mother's advice inspired him to release a string of curses aimed at my father's shortsightedness, including a lengthy riff labeling him a "blind bastard," a designation that caused my mother to laugh aloud, an unfamiliar merriness that shocked Henry into silence.

---

For the first eight years of his life, you see, my father had been completely blind, the result of an embryonic virus that had prevented a crucial optical synapse from developing. His affliction did not seem to slow him down. By all accounts, he was a remarkably outgoing child, if something of a wise-ass, and both adults and other children tended to indulge him and consider him more clever than he probably was. Then, inexplicably, around his eighth birthday, he discerned floating shapes drifting across the field of his right eye. Within a few days,

< 55 >

little starbursts of light erupted, cracking the black expanse, and in their wake, a peculiarly angular world rapidly came into focus. Soon his left eye offered the same cloudy frame that had preceded vision in the other eye, and in an even more expedient fashion, that eye's vision too raced from the vague to the precise. Remarkably, the missing connectors had tremored their own way into being.

I can hardly imagine what that must have been like, discovering an entirely new dimension of life. It must have been almost as if he had realized he could fly, really and truly, outside his dreams. Miraculous, yes, but disconcerting, too. Extroverted as a blind child, my father became increasingly reticent as his vision lightened and splintered abruptly into the twin unimaginables of color and illumination. He'd been interpreting both all his life, twisting the visual descriptions he'd been given into his own sightless spectrum:

red, the feel of silk between his finger;

green, the loamy scent of a spring day on a baseball field;

yellow, a bit of runny egg gelling on his tongue.

His mother's hand smoothing the heat of his always wild hair from his forehead—well, this was as good a definition of light as he had known.

While he attempted to reconcile his former world with that transformed by sight, my father could barely talk, he was so agitated by nameless desire. He wondered what else he'd missed, what else he was still missing. How so much of what he had perceived could have been so wrong. He begged for twilight car rides just so he could stare into homes in those dusky hours when lamps had been lit, the curtains not yet drawn, and family life presented as a tableau for public viewing. Occasionally, too, his nagging fascination drove him to steal a trinket from another house or a stranger's pocket.

Did he need those things? Those Hummel figurines in their lederhosen. Those dented sailing trophies or knitted infant caps nestled in

< 56 >

tissue? Did he even want them? The slot cars or carved ivory cigarette cases or toy German pistols? He couldn't say. Still, he stole steadily from the time he was ten, and although he'd had a few close calls, until now he had never been discovered.

He relayed his criminal history—embellished, of course, with unfettered daring—to Dr. Alice Chase, his company-appointed psychologist, who was required to keep a record of their conversations. Weekly, he asked for his own copy, which he kept in his underwear drawer, right where anyone could find it, slip it under his shirt, and take it to the bathroom to read. Dr. Alice had her own thoughts, of course, on my father's thievery. How, *perhaps*—Dr. Alice always couched her slightest opinions in conjectures, as if she were afraid to be sued for having a real opinion—how *possibly* my father's greatest wish was to be caught, to force people to see him differently just as he'd been forced once to re-vision them.

*Maybe,* my father agreed.

He seemed to make every effort to be amicable during his therapy sessions, but anyone reading these accounts could tell my father had been hoping for something else from Alice Chase, a reprisal of his boyhood miracle, the world rearranging itself and carrying him along. I imagined he asked her for something—a glass of water, a fresh tissue—using that moment of inattention to swipe the fountain pen that he'd taped to his transcript. Then he might have risen to his feet, refusing her prescription for Xanax, since, he would have said with a sigh, life in bucolic Clementsville offered him not the slightest amount of stress, a statement I would have liked to argue with him.

———

Although our parents had owned their house since our first year at Holt, Henry and I were in no way part of Clementsville, a town that I decided, from my reading of the local paper, was overrun by a single family. Loreckis manned the fire department, the garbage trucks, and the local post office. Joe Lorecki was the chief of police; his younger brother and nephew were patrolmen. Goldiane Lorecki, an ancient black-clad widow, styled hair at the Lorecki Salon with her son, Albert. Marco Lorecki tended bar at the High Spot Tavern, a place rumored to sell alcohol to anyone who could peer over the counter. Janice Lorecki taught first grade at St Cecilia's, and Father Lorecki always took the early mass. All the Loreckis lived within the six blocks that comprised the core of Clementsville.

Our parents' house, on the other hand, lay on five acres up a long hidden graveled drive and faced away from town towards the open fields that signaled estate country. Part stone, part clapboard, the house was a Revolutionary War relic with narrow doorways so low that Henry and I were forever ducking or slamming our foreheads against the lintels. A pervasive smell of mold and wood smoke hung about our usually unused rooms and made my nostrils itch continually. Our doors didn't even have doorknobs. They closed with black iron latches that made a loud, disturbing click. And because the original renovators had been stingy with electrical outlets, the rooms were also poorly lit. I had grown used to florescent dorm rooms and the routine rumble of shared lives. It was difficult to adjust, to stave off an expectant feeling in Clementsville, as if we were waiting for a forgotten door to burst open and illuminate our new dim lives.

Yet I was awed at my unexpected good fortune. At Holt, where I'd been halfway through my sophomore year, the push for success was palpable and judgment permeated every waking moment. In contrast, competition at Clementsville High was pallid. I was far ahead in both math and English. And, although I was late for the season, the Clementsville basketball team had suffered an alarming number of season-busting injuries, and I was allowed to substitute, playing an ordinary but enthusiastic forward. The combination of good grades

< 58 >

and sports acumen was enough to make me into something of a boy wonder, a role so new to me that I floated through my schooldays, half-afraid I would wake up soon and discover I was a colossal dupe, strung out on psilocybin mushrooms, which in the past had suffused me with unwarranted and overwhelming feelings of well-being and caused me to perform certain feats that I afterwards regretted and always denied.

As for Henry—he revamped his senior schedule altogether, claiming he'd met all graduation requirements and needed just six more simple credits. He took shop, bonehead history, and an English class bordering on remedial. He also signed up for art although he hadn't touched so much as a crayon since our preschool days. For his PE requirement, he chose weight-lifting. He would have bowed and taken French, but the school didn't offer a class for his talents.

"How sad," he told our mother. "Clementsville has no French 8."

Within a couple of weeks, Henry even had new friends: huge muscle-bound losers with tattoos. It was as if he had entered prison instead of public high school. It seemed to me that the two of us had been finally been dropped into a more appropriate sorter than Holt and if I, in all my shiny slender eagerness, now slid amongst the dimes, Henry tumbled headlong toward the heavy-shouldered nickels.

---

Henry's new best friend was Davy Lorecki, the son of the construction Lorecki. Rico Lorecki trucks rumbled through town and parked outside Geneva Lorecki's Sweet Pickle Deli at every mealtime. Davy's mother was Arista Lorecki, a woman known far and wide as the Statue Lady. A girl at school told me Arista's sculptures haunted the Loreckis' house. They hunkered over tables, crouched in stairwells, leaned against mantels. On the weekends, Henry began helping Lorecki deliver Arista's sculptures, shrouded in layers of packing, to

< 59 >

galleries in New Hope or out on Long Island. She paid them twenty dollars each for the delivery. Easy work, but Lorecki could make twice that working for his old man, and he was sick of wasting his time. Within a few weeks of their acquaintance, Lorecki offered to give my brother an old van of his uncle's, on the condition that my brother take over Arista's deliveries. Of course, Henry might need a hand with the deliveries. The statues weren't that heavy, just ungainly. Almost anyone would do as a helper. Here Lorecki paused and gave me his dubious attention: "Even Puss here," he said. Henry shrugged off Lorecki until the Friday night when neither my mother's Audi nor my father's Volvo was in the driveway and he had to walk the two and a half miles to the High Spot Tavern. The next afternoon my new basketball team had an away game. As our bus paused at Clementsville's single traffic light, I caught sight of Henry and Lorecki, idling in an ancient Ford Econoline outside the drugstore, Henry in the driver's seat. I knew my brother had made his decision. His new vehicle was the same painfully bright blue used to paint the Holt pool. Along the side panels, swimming out from under the thin brush paint job, were the words:

*Beecham's Champion Pearl-Diving Team*
and beneath them:
*Pearl Diving—America's fastest-growing sport.*

I could imagine my parents' reactions. "I once did a little pearl diving myself," my father would say when he saw it the next day. My mother would merely purse her lips into a knife edge of a smile, and it would be easy to see she'd blame my father for the van as well.

I was still thinking about Henry's acquisition later that night, when after yet another humiliating defeat, the coach tried to cheer us up by having the bus driver make an unscheduled stop at the grocery store in the Colonial Shopping Center in Beecham, the next town over from Clementsville and the one-time home of Henry's new van.

It was nearly eleven o'clock. We were too loud in the parking lot, our voices cracking against the cold air. Inside, the throbbing overhead lights and the abrupt swoosh of the electric door at our backs dazed us. At one point, I nearly blacked out and, on recovering, glanced around to see if anyone had noticed. The checkers continued to banter with customers; stock clerks kept shoveling boxes on shelves; my teammates raised havoc among the snack foods. In the aisle directly before me, an ox of a woman, her head lowered, pulled two full carts. And, behind her, my handsome, oblivious father, his face rapt with concentration, slipped a carton of cigarettes inside his overcoat.

By the time he reached the checkstand, I was out the door and halfway to the bus. There I waited, ducking low when, holding a tiny paper bag in his fist, my father sauntered to the pea green Volvo sedan he drove to the train station each morning.

Henry was still out when I arrived home. My mother was sleeping the exhausted open-mouthed sleep of the justly maligned who had downed too much vermouth. And my father was comfortably slumped in his usual plaid wing chair, engrossed in a television movie about a pair of gunslingers, and eating pistachios from the paper bag. He looked disheveled and boyish in the blue light of the television, like any number of dateless Holt boys on a Saturday night, but he brightened when he saw me and held the little paper bag out.

"Don't know what came over me tonight, I had an overwhelming yen for pistachios," he said, spitting a shell into his palm. "You can buy them just like this," he said. "Alice told me about this. Bulk, she calls it. Makes me feel as if I'm really at the movies."

"That's popcorn, Dad," I said. "You buy popcorn, not nuts, at the movies."

"Yes, that's right," he said, happily splitting a shell with his teeth. "Popcorn. See that fellow," he pointed to an actor, dressed like Tecumseh, the cigar-store Indian. "I went to school with him."

"Oh, yeah?" I said. "What's his name?" The credits were due to roll in a minute.

My father didn't miss a beat: "Harold Cloudsplitter, then," he said. "Not sure what he's calling himself these days." He paused to pick a piece of shell from his mouth. "Good game, tonight?"

I shrugged, not sure truth would have any place in this conversation.

"That's all right, Kenny," my father said, rattling his pistachio bag in commiseration. "There's always a second act, trust me."

Watching my father with his tousled charm and carefree wisdom, I was suddenly bitterly certain that of all our family, I'd been the most wronged. Henry had Lorecki and his crew, of course. My father, his Dr. Alice Chase. Even my mother was comforted by her cocktails and stories. Only the thought of my errant cousin, the floundering Laura, soothed me. I imagined her as I was, alone and disregarded, out of place in whatever new world her mother had decided to drop her.

———————

She arrived unheralded. I saw her first in the halls of Clementsville High School. My mother's fragile relationship with her sister had derailed again when Ginny accused her of rewriting the past. By then, however, my aunt had come up with a plan for Laura that included Clementsville and her old school friend, Kay Croyton. The Croytons were old money and lived in an estate out on Leyland Road. Aunt Ginny, having just entered a new love affair, couldn't break herself away, but she'd arranged an illusion of caretaking by sending our cousin to live with the Croytons in proximity to us, her true family.

"Typical," my mother fumed. "You would think she would have at least asked if Laura could stay here. And Laura! Not one phone call! I haven't seen her since she was five years old, and she couldn't be bothered to let me know she was here."

The next moment she was on the phone to Kay Croyton, her voice transformed into silk. "Of course," my mother was saying. "Well, yes, that's Ginny, you know." Her laugh was icy.

To us, my mother was more direct: "Kay Croyton's a drunken idiot. She hardly realizes that Laura's there. 'We gave her the carriage house,' she says. What the hell is Ginny thinking?"

My mother drove directly to the Croyton estate where she was met at Laura's door by a nearly naked man who claimed to speak little English and was apparently extremely rude.

"What did I expect? The way that girl's been raised?" She threw her leather gloves onto the hall table as if she were tossing away any further thoughts about Laura. But you could tell she thought Laura might be caught in another of her situations, that maybe the savage at the door had prevented my cousin from acknowledging my mother. She sent my father back out to Leyland Road to gauge the level of Laura's distress. He was gone for nearly two hours and arrived home wearing a rakish red-and-black-striped wool scarf I did not recognize. Still, my father didn't have much to say about his visit. Laura had been alone. She'd given him a cup of coffee.

"She's fine, Elaine," he said, finally. "More than fine."

An understatement, as it turned out.

Clementsville High was not a small school, but my cousin immediately garnered attention. Slim, with full, round breasts, the left slightly larger than the right, she favored black V-neck cashmere sweaters and short black skirts that made her long legs appear even more shapely and elongated. Laura spent her free periods in a corner of the cafeteria, chewing on a nicotine inhaler and reading Mishima in Japanese. Her skin was incredibly white, without a single blemish, her straight black hair cut as short as a boy's. She looked like a woman out of black-and-white movie. Everyone tried to hit on her: jocks, potheads, the theater crowd, even the vice-principal, Mr. Nugent,

< 63 >

followed her languorous swish through the halls as if waiting for an infraction that would allow him to call her into his private office. Although I knew we were cousins, we hadn't seen each other since we were children, and I never spoke to her. Neither did Henry as far as I knew. Despite her checkered school career, Laura had somehow vaulted ahead of me and she was between us, a junior.

On the afternoon we turned in our basketball jerseys, I realized I'd left my backpack and a particularly important assignment in my English classroom. Of all the Clementsville teachers, my English teacher, Jason Donner, clung most to the notion that his class mattered to us and our futures. He was a few inches shorter than me, but his shoulders were broader, his pectorals monstrous. Rumor maintained that he was an Ironman junkie who spent his weekends lifting in competitions. If that were true, he worked hard to lead us all astray. He kept his curly brown hair neatly trimmed and sported unfashionable aviator glasses above his thin white nose. He wore cabled sweater vests, and his voice trembled whenever his interpretations of Mark Twain or William Golding were challenged. Any life Jason Donner might have beyond his classroom was unimaginable to me, so I had a reasonable hope that he would still be there, that the classroom would be open. The halls were deserted and seemed in their emptiness longer than they did in the crowded breaks between classes. I sprinted and arrived at the door out of breath, hearing only my own heartbeat in my ears. The door was shut but unlocked, and I did not hesitate,

Donner knelt on the floor, his head in the lap of my cousin Laura, who reclined in the chair behind his desk. He jumped when the door squealed open and offered me the startled half-seeing look of a dog whose territory had been invaded.

"What the hell do you want?" he said.

Laura rolled back in his chair and rearranged her skirt, which was twisted around her hips. She brushed at her knees.

< 64 >

"Hey, Kenny," she said, easily.

"Laura," I said, my voice matching hers in nonchalance. You'd think we ate lunch together every day.

My pack lay beside a desk over by the window. I made my way through the desks and snatched it, banging it heavily against my hip as I raced back to the door.

"Sorry," I said.

"Wait," Laura said. I hovered by the open door, trying not to see Jason Donner's anguish as she leaned down to pick up her own black leather pack, revealing an inch of pearly skin at her waist. My own heart beat rapidly as if I'd just witnessed an accident.

She turned toward him finally. "Kenny is my cousin."

"Your cousin?" Donner said, staring at me.

"Yes," I answered, miserably.

Henry was waiting outside in the van. As a favor to our mother, he picked me up from practice and he was watching when Laura and I left the building, when she kissed me on the lips, and murmured, "Thanks. Your family's good at helping me out of messy situations." I was too stunned to ask her what I'd done or, more precisely, what my family had done. The touch of her lips had sent a cold shock down my legs, and I automatically moved my backpack in front of me to hide the erection I knew was coming. She didn't wait around, just shrugged before heading toward the teacher's parking lot where she kept the silver Karmann Ghia that once belonged to the Croytons' horse trainer.

Henry didn't say a word as we left the school. At the first traffic light, he glanced in the rear view mirror, then began whistling softly.

"Our cousin," I said, "Laura."

"Uh-huh," he said, lighting a joint. "I've seen her at the High Spot."

"You talk?"

He paused for a long toke and choked out: "Lorecki tried."

"Jesus, Henry, Lorecki?"

The light flicked from red to green as Henry gunned the van's engine to keep it from stalling. As we rumbled through the intersection, his eyes shifted to the rear view mirror and the Karmann Ghia making its neat, quick turn away from us.

Two days later, Laura was in the van when Henry arrived to pick me up from track practice. I saw her white face from a distance, framed in the Econoline's front window, and I thought for a moment that Henry had put one of Arista's sculptures in the front seat—she was so poised and removed. Henry told me later they'd finally talked at the High Spot, and I have no reason not to believe him, but I don't. I think he went out to the Croytons' estate the evening he saw Laura kiss me.

It was Laura, not me, who took over for Davy, helping Henry deliver Arista's shrouded sculptures. They would leave early on Saturday morning and be gone all day. The van, once permeated with the mingled stench of sea salt and mold and pot smoke, now reeked of sex.

"She's our cousin," I yelled at Henry one evening out of nowhere.

"Yeah, so?"

"So, you can't sleep with your cousin."

"Kenny," my brother said, calmly. "When did you become such a dick brain?"

And yet I wasn't the only one. Even my father noticed, pulling me into the kitchen one evening to inquire if I accompanied Henry and Laura on the deliveries, if they were seeing a lot of each other, if Henry ever brought along a girlfriend. And then there was Jason Donner. At first, my English teacher merely trailed Henry and Laura in the halls. We looked alike even then—all the males in our family, even my forty-six-year-old father, have the same lanky build—and he must have figured out that Henry and I were brothers.

"He'll treat it like a logic problem," Laura said. "If Henry and

< 66 >

Kenny are brothers and Kenny is Laura's cousin, then Henry, too, must be Laura's cousin."

We were huddled in the van's front seat, while Henry collected his weekly pay and instructions from Arista Lorecki. Davy's mother was not a woman who rushed. We'd been waiting for Henry in the Loreckis' driveway for ten minutes already, and the van windows were almost completely fogged, lending a covert intimacy to our conversation that I cherished. Laura was wearing an old gray cashmere sweater Henry had filched from my father, and she passed the time by idly sucking on the cuffs until they hung over her hands, misshapen and damp. Her pretty lips had reddened with the effort.

"Your brother knows Jason's harmless," Laura said, pinching a bit of sweater fuzz from her tongue.

Twice Donner had nearly caught Henry smoking his noonday bowl of hash. He'd become a nasty shadow, slipping out of his classroom and roaming the parking lot during Henry's free period. Just yesterday, he slammed me against the lockers in the hall outside the language lab after school and grabbed my shoulders hard.

"Oh, sorry, Kenny," he stammered, when he saw my face. "I thought..."

I didn't wait for him to finish. I knew what he thought, a great hulk of a guy practically bawling.

"C'mon," Laura said, "let's walk around. My legs are so cold, I can hardly feel them."

The light outside the van seemed harsh and disorienting. Squinting, I followed Laura along the Loreckis' high back fence, nearly falling over her when we reached the gate. The backyard materialized before us just as my vision began to clear.

A party was in progress. Naked women of all shapes and sizes, linked in groups, crouched in the flowerbeds, on their knees, creamy

< 67 >

hands held out in supplication. More women peeked from between the fir trees at the yard's far border, another one balanced starkly behind a shed window, her white palm raised against the dirty glass. It became a game. As each figure came into focus, I discovered another gem rising from the ordinary grit of a backyard landscape. I have no idea how long I stood there, lost in the fantasy, hoping one of the women would look up, smile, and invite me to join them. It wasn't until Laura wandered into their midst that I snapped awake and realized that, of course, these must be Arista's statues. Yet even as I acknowledged that indisputable fact, my heart pounded, and I wondered again if I was being deceived. The statues gave off a suppressed energy as if they were real women who had just landed within my grasp and were only pretending to be unreachable.

"They're beautiful," I blurted.

Laura gazed at me with amusement. She strolled back to me, grinning, and draped her arms around my neck. She leaned into me, brushing her polished cheek against my rough one.

"You are going to be such a sweet man," she whispered, and I felt foolishly elated until in the next breath, she said, with real affection in her voice, "Jason should see these. He'd go crazy."

As if she'd summoned him, Donner suddenly rounded the corner in his Volvo. I recognized the distinctive tick of the Volvo engine, so like my father's station car, and I jumped, but Laura held me. A mere moment later, the Loreckis' front door slammed. Laura raised her head, but kept her arms around me. I turned around just in time to see both faces tighten as if Donner and Henry were each connected to Laura by a string she'd just pulled taut.

---

By early June, my parents had settled into a surprisingly comfortable niche. My mother hurdled her anger, put away the vermouth bottle,

< 68 >

and decided to open a gallery, the first in Clementsville. Already, she'd contacted Arista Lorecki, wooing her with an account of her premarital art history courses at Sarah Lawrence, her keen networking skills, and an amusing story about her failed career as an artist's model.

According to my father's Alice Chase log, he too kept himself busy all spring. He'd stolen more cigarettes, a dozen unopened cartons stashed in the cupboard under the stairs. And flashlights and beef jerky. He'd gone completely against character and flirted with the Lorecki girls in order to pilfer penny candy from the bin inside the drugstore. Twists of bubblegum and loose Tootsie rolls weighed down the pockets of his old plaid jacket. He sauntered off on evening walks and returned with lawn ornaments and license plate holders. But all this suburban marauding ended when he tried lifting a box of spark plugs from Nickel's Garage. In Tommy Nickel (Gussie Lorecki's husband), my father found the answer to his problem. Tommy held his hand out for the spark plugs as if he'd just asked my father to pick them up for him.

"You don't need to do that, son," he told my father, gently.

There was a girl at Tommy Nickel's shop that afternoon—probably Tommy's granddaughter, I thought—and my father told Alice Chase how he gazed from the wrinkled, unshaven face of Tommy Nickel to the sweet curve of the girl's white cheek and felt something inside him unravel. The light altered as if trees had been felled all around him or a huge amorphous and opaque skein had slipped away. He knew, of course, that he didn't *need* a box of spark plugs any more than he *needed* cigarettes or Tootsie rolls, but when Tommy Nickel placed a hand on my father's shoulder and steered him toward the door, he thought he could finally see what it was he did lack. My father felt real affection in that gesture, in the calloused weight of Tommy's hand, and conceded that what he'd been searching for in all his thievery was simple human connection.

"Perhaps your wife?" Alice Chase asked. "Your sons?"

My father shook his head. Didn't she see? It was colors all over again.

He had lived in a bubble until he had taken up a box of pins and now, now, he could see the hues of passion, the subtle illumination of desire that had eluded him. There was more he wanted, so much more he needed to take. Yet, it was clear that what he so desperately wanted could not be eased away so neatly. His pockets weren't big enough to claim what was becoming an insatiable longing.

*Desire. Passion.*

Reading my father's account, I experienced my own revelation. And pins, I realized with a pleasant shock, weren't all that hard to come by.

———————

Henry and Laura began squabbling just before graduation. It didn't take much to get them going: a whispered insult, a misunderstood tug on the hair. Just good-natured teasing, at first ending in embarrassing tickling fights or a spatter of silly apologies. More than a few times that last month, Laura wasn't able to accompany Henry on his Arista deliveries, and when he returned in the late afternoon, he couldn't find her. She had never been keen on coming to our house, where my mother would relentlessly interrogate her about Ginny. She didn't even like to telephone. A couple of times, Henry wouldn't even see Laura from Friday evening until Monday morning when we arrived, on schedule, to pick her up for school.

Then, one morning, while Henry was struggling to light the end of a joint, I glimpsed the square back end of a car speeding away from the Croytons' driveway as we approached.

"Can you believe it?" I said to Henry, my voice rich with incredulous naiveté. "What's Donner doing out here so early in the morning?"

Henry went to get Laura and stayed inside the carriage house until

I was sure we'd be late. Eventually, they came outside and got into the van. Laura barely nodded at me. The ride to school was utterly silent. As we passed the teachers' parking lot, Henry muttered under his breath.

"Fuck you," Laura said.

"I'd have to stand in line," he answered flatly, and she flew out of the van.

That same afternoon, the parked van was totaled, brutally broadsided while Henry practiced graduation ceremonies with his class. Laura telephoned later that evening, but Henry was already cruising with Davy in Lorecki's Charger, hunting for Donner.

"She said to tell you you're a paranoid bastard," I told Henry later.

They seemed exactly the right words at the time.

It was Donner who tracked down Henry around closing time at the High Spot. Gone were the sweater vest, the awkward glasses, the air of frustrated haplessness. At first Henry didn't know the bulky stranger who advanced on him, but Marco Lorecki, the bartender, took one glance at the tattoos that circled the newcomer's massive forearms and biceps and recognized him as kin.

"Take that shit outside," he told Donner, sending them to the alley to fight like couple of lust-crazed toms.

Lorecki came in at the end, but you'd have to call the fight a draw. Henry with his battered face. Donner weeping into his bloodied fists. And Laura kissing no one's wounds.

She didn't come to graduation, and Henry celebrated without her, as perhaps only I knew he could. A couple of letters addressed to him were unfortunately mislaid. I heard a rumor she was leaving any day to live with her father in Baltimore. She telephoned again, but my father beat me to the phone that time. I heard him breathe her name, or thought I did, but he didn't mention the call to Henry, who strolled into the house almost the minute my father replaced the receiver.

That same afternoon, I noticed the Volvo's driver's door was ajar and when I went to close it, I spied a folded white square lying on the front seat. I flicked it open, saw Laura's familiar slanted handwriting, and slipped the note into my pocket. You would have thought she'd know Henry never drove that car.

That night I woke just after midnight, breathless and sweating, as if I'd been sealed in a box. I had forgotten to turn on the attic fan, and my room was stifling. Two floors down, I paused in Henry's doorway, envying him his easy slumber. My lucky brother. In sleep, he appeared as perfect as perhaps he had once been. The curtains sighed with the warm night breeze, the moon was nearly full, and the house filled with the sort of blue light that made the molecules in everything not only visible, but essential and beautifully deceptive. Bands of white moonlight slashed across the black polished wood surfaces, and I thought of Laura and felt again her cheek against mine, the weight of her body leaning into me.

*Come to me*, her note had implored. *Tonight.*

The ride up Leyland Road was the path through the woods in a dozen fairy tales. Trees sighed overhead. A family of deer posed gravely as my bike whirled past. The road rippled beneath my bike tires. Where the blacktop broke and gave way to gravel at the end of Leyland Road and the deep dusty ruts of the private drives began, I stashed my bike behind the crumbling stone pillars of the Croyton estate and found the trail through the field. Bright eyes appeared at every turn, skittering field mice, lazy opossums, shambling, guilty-looking raccoons—more deer, grazing on the moonlit leaves of the abandoned orchards.

Like Henry's sleeping face, the earth had been sweetened, every blemish smoothed. I nearly forgot why I'd come. I thought instead of going on past the stone pillars and Laura's toward Lord's Lake, where

< 72 >

a solitary rowboat lapped beside a dock belonging to the Catholic retreat house there. My mission seemed meaningless in the face of the night before me. The morning meant nothing; only the mesmerized calm of the night claimed me, and I walked and walked until, abruptly, the path narrowed. The high grasses by the fence scratched my bare legs as I stepped into the stable drive and the sound of my footfalls began chipping rudely at the still night air.

The carriage house lay in front of me. Standing in the gravel drive in my T-shirt and boxers, I gazed up at her open bedroom window. As I wondered whether I should wake Laura or simply retrace my route, the side door of the carriage house opened and a figure slipped out and ran towards me. Time inverted itself in that magic way that occurs when light is no longer the guidepost, and at first I merely observed as if the figure were advancing from a far distance. I did not recognize Laura, although I'm sure I must have known it was she, but I did not hesitate when she came into my arms, her nakedness such a shock that a cold shiver came over me and my teeth actually chattered. Her mouth was on mine before she realized her mistake.

"Oh, Kenny," she said, "it's you."

For a moment, I thought she would run away again, flounce that magnificent body back to the carriage house. As my vision adjusted to the subtle illuminations of the night, I could see her expression shift rapidly from anticipation to resignation to something harder, more calculated, but she held me tightly by the hand and led me to a spot behind the hedgerow where a nest of silky blankets had been spread. The mosquitoes were fierce those early weeks of summer, but I noticed nothing as we fell together. I had never had the whole of a girl's bare skin against mine before and the feeling, like diving through water, was so overwhelming, I struggled to hold onto consciousness. Her skin was cool, a brilliant white, and smelled of dirt after a long, hard rain. Who knows where desire starts or how one moment a person can be pleasantly weary, enthralled by silence and solitude, and the next, pulled ravenously beneath the surface. Too soon we moved apart, and I plunged into sleep, feeling my arms spread wide as I let the world go.

When morning arrived, gray-shadowed and damp. I woke rolled into the dew-soaked blankets—alone and shivering. The sound of a retreating car heading down the gravel driveway made me conscious of my nakedness. I kept my head down, hurried into my damp underclothes and sneakers, and lit off through the field. A new crowd was out: cows, rabbits, cats on the hunt, all of them oblivious to my passage through their world. At the stone pillars, I retrieved my bike and pedaled furiously home, hardly noticing as light reclaimed the world, bush by bush, tree by tree. Everything falling back into place.

# TWO GIRLS OFF QUARRY ROAD

Everyone knew about Cleo Talmadge. At eight, she roamed barefoot among the dusty, troublesome Knutson boys from Quarry Road. With her cropped hair and dirty T-shirt and jeans, she was nearly indistinguishable from those tow-headed Finns. The Knutsons liked to shout out random guttural words that couldn't help but appear insulting, and she quickly learned to mimic them. She walked like them too—lanky and insolent, tilted to one side with a wide boy-like stance. But unlike the Finns, who considered everything one beat too long, hesitation was never one of Cleo Talmadge's flaws. In fact, she had a talent for disappearing, like the time there was that drowning in the quarry, the sad end of some misconceived contest with a pair of visiting kids, or the afternoon when the Finns set fire to the caretaker's shack while playing with their homemade explosives. All of them were rounded up. You bet they hadn't taken the chance to flee. But the only sign of Cleo was a plastic barrette the Finns' mother had given her, a pink kitten on a metal clip the boys had used to secure the fuse. No one ratted on her—the Finns said they'd *found* the barrette—but she avoided the quarry for a long time after that. The Finns weren't ever going to look up in time. Even at eight, Cleo figured that out.

As she grew, Cleo's reputation corrupted further. She made people uneasy. She prowled yards late at night, teasing dogs into barking frenzies. Don Crepp, who delivered papers before dawn, caught her for a moment in his headlights as she perched on the low roof of an uptown garage. And, well past midnight, a bone-weary visiting nurse nearly drove into Cleo as the girl scattered handfuls of pilfered apple

< 75 >

blossoms across the empty downtown intersection. She was just a child, but although no one could prove a thing, it wasn't long before all sorts of irregularities were blamed on her: the theft of lawn furniture, broken bottles by the bank drive-through, rosebushes stripped of their blossoms, even missing gutters.

Her parents were no help: Alicia and Tim Talmadge. Postal carriers, the pair of them, their routes bumping up against each other. They left before six each morning and walked the few blocks to the brick post office, sipping on a shared mug of milky coffee. Side by side, they packed their mailbags, setting up their routes together. On their days off, always coordinated, they labored in their pristine garden, shoulders almost touching as they knelt to feed rhodies and azaleas, or charged through one household chore after another. They tidied the garage, oiled door hinges. They starched and ironed bedding, put away preserves and filled birdfeeders. They were minding a nest in the wind's path. Afterward, they would sit down to a simple dinner: a pair of braised cutlets, potatoes, peas. They set the table, almost always forgetting the third place until Cleo appeared, trailing mud and bits of gravel over their newly waxed floor.

Little of their careful regard went towards the girl. They picked up her messes, washed her clothes, and fed her when she appeared. Beyond that, they were at a loss. After all, they'd known and loved each other since junior high, while Cleo was a newcomer, a interloper, whose presence in their union would always be a surprise—no, a downright shock—as if they'd never imagined they could be so invaded. And although they went through the motions the first few years, the child upended their ease, and they could not help resenting her from almost her first infant squalls. To be perfectly honest, they were relieved when she began to wander.

Which she did almost as soon as she could walk, as if she knew right away she had no place in the bungalow built for two. Cleo simply appeared—in kitchens, kneeling on a high counter, her paw in a cupboard, or on a back porch, squatting over a planter she'd improvised as a potty. She might have been scooped up by Social Services (and most would argue she should have been) if it hadn't been for her grandfather. Once the neighbors realized Alicia's father was Harry Kane, the contractor who built half the town and owned a good bit of it still, they dialed his number every time the little girl showed up.

My brother Ed worked for Harry Kane, and according to him, Harry genuinely liked the little girl. They were friends of a sort. While Alicia had irritated the hell out of Harry with her endless industry, that tiresome juvenile romance, from the first fit Cleo pitched in his kitchen, he was won over. Her indifference to his own raging tickled him. No one else could approach Kane when he had his dander up. And you couldn't ignore the look of her, of course—the lazy green eyes, that gold flyaway hair.

"She's the spitting image of Kitty," my brother declared, referring to Kane's first wife, a local girl who had died from septic shock when Alicia was in grammar school. Kitty Kane's likeness embellished every one of the company trucks. Maybe it was that—the constant presence of Cleo's familiar image on those loud, brash trucks, always running across curbs and shearing off tree branches as they raced from lumberyard to job site—that made her the obvious culprit for every local misdeed.

In the end, though, even Harry Kane wasn't about to chase after Cleo. The girl amused him, and she was welcome in his house—he even let her sleep in the shrine of Kitty's sewing room—but he'd been done raising kids a long time back, and he wasn't about to pick up the yoke again, attending to every busybody's yelping.

"What's *your* problem?" he'd demand of any complaining caller before wordlessly disconnecting and sending one of his men to pick up Cleo. He was more ticked off at the callers than at his granddaughter.

< 77 >

She'd be fine if they all left her alone. That was the key with the Kanes. Eventually, they all found their own way out, even if it wasn't pretty.

Surprisingly, Kane never received a single call from the school. Aside from a tendency toward daydreaming, Cleo never caused a lick of trouble there.

"I think she comes here to rest," her favorite teacher, Sandra Daly, once mused to her colleagues in the teachers' lounge.

Beau Chase, who taught seventh grade math, lit a cigarette, squinted at the smoke, and on the exhale, said, "I can relate."

"I just wish she'd connect a little," Sandra Daly lamented.

Except for the Finns, Cleo didn't have anyone she might call a friend until the sixth grade, when Katie Schwinger moved to town. It was Katie who kept Cleo coming to school, the teachers reckoned.

"She woke the kid up," Beau Chase would say later. "Anchored her."

"Katie loved Cleo," Sandra said. "I don't think Cleo got over that. She let her guard down with Katie."

---

*Poor Katie.* That was everyone's first impression of the new kid who had come to live with her great aunt and uncle way out on Quarry Road, past the Knutson place and even beyond that of the quarryman's widow. The Schwingers lived clear on the other side of the quarry itself. Katie wouldn't have cared about the isolation. Like Cleo, she had been left on her own for most of her young life, so much, in fact, that she'd home-schooled herself, using the newspaper and television and the monthly bookmobile from the county library. As a consequence, she'd inadvertently advanced, testing into the eighth grade, though she was almost a year and a half younger than the rest of them.

Small, bespectacled, with thin brown hair and a noticeable overbite, Katie might have been an object of ridicule if it weren't for her serenity, a deep-set quality of acceptance that made everyone around her feel a little bit better about themselves. It was as if Katie had seen the whole of her life and set her shoulder against the task the way a tired man might undertake a long walk home, and the rest of us were easing by, albeit shabbily, in our old cars.

A poor little orphan girl, people decided. Someone had set her straight about her prospects, and she was that odd creature: a practical child, abandoned. And, although most people applauded the Schwingers for taking the girl in, there was one notable exception. Katie's second cousin, Curtis Schwinger, a clerk at the courthouse, was vocally upset his folks had become involved, intimating Katie's tragedy wasn't so clear-cut. Who knew, Curtis said, but that one day some released felon might come to claim her and take issue with the way the aunt and uncle had swept her off.

"I've seen her kind of people," he would say, conveniently ignoring the fact that he and the girl had blood between them.

Every day, he witnessed real bottom-feeders shuffling through the courthouse, throwing tantrums in the holding room, stinking of piss and random venom. More than once, he'd been called to subdue a drug-addled maniac, all that high-pitched wailing and feet kicking at the stale courthouse air. The hellish drama. They always tried to bite him with their broken yellow teeth as if they truly were animals.

They were all over the place, he'd learned, this subclass, cooking up trouble in their dingy country trailers and broken-down bungalows, where day and night melded and horrible, nonsensical plans hatched.

"Just listen to the police scanner any night of the week," Curtis advised: "*Couple at Ernie's Motor Court; Woman Behind Valley View Apartments.* These aren't simple burglaries being called in, you know.

"They're armed to the teeth, too," he went on. Sometimes, they squirreled in weapons inexpertly concealed on their bodies, and Curtis had to actually touch them, shaking out greasy guns or sticky knives from the stiff folds of their gruesome clothing and personally conveying these weapons to the evidence room. Katie, he knew, had been whisked out of a notorious trailer park. He'd rooted out the paperwork and recognized the address. After a few beers at the Courthouse Tavern, he would worry openly about strangers arriving in the night, bouncing down the lonely potholed road to unearth the bundles of folded paper money and bank receipts he supposed his mother and dad still hid in buried tomato juice cans across the property, money he intended to inherit one day. He wasn't insensible, either, to Katie's friendship with Cleo.

"Look at the company she keeps," he'd declare, as if he were one of the lawyers he watched daily, the kind who make Big Points no one could dispute. He didn't seem to mind who was sitting at the bar. He'd spool out all kinds of baloney about the nefarious schemes of his schoolgirl cousin and her ilk. My brother Ed and some of the other fellows who drove Kane's big trucks frequented the tavern, and eventually, one of them would steer Curtis off his stool and out onto Bay Street where the smack of the wind off the water would stir him and seem to clear his head. He had an apartment in one of the Victorians two streets up, and no one much minded seeing him home. Better that than let him slip away, half-howling about injustice. His parents had been roused more than a few times in the night, their kitchen table pounded and dishes rattled as Curtis berated their blinkered judgment. His father would make him coffee, his mother would dish out pie; they did their best to soothe him. Then one night poor Katie had awakened to Curtis cursing and stumbling around in her bedroom, looking, he later claimed, for his own belongings, for that had been his childhood room, another theft for which he held Katie responsible. As his appalled mother comforted Katie, his father sent Curtis on his way with an uncharacteristic sharpness in the elder Schwinger's

< 80 >

voice that made it clear, to Curtis at least, who was welcome in that household and who was not.

Despite all Curtis's worrying, Katie was a model child. She did her chores as well as any adult and without complaint. She had a heartfelt affinity for her relatives' animals—a dog named Steven Schwinger, four cats, a tiny Nubian goat—and was more help than hindrance to the older couple. She gave them so little to worry about that they didn't mind Cleo coming around at all, despite the talk in town. They were glad, in fact, their Katie had such a dear friend. She was such a homebody. The only time anyone saw Katie on her own was either at the library or marching down their long dirt road to unload the mail from the metal box on the county road. Usually, she'd be reading a book as she walked, followed by Grady, the goat, and a bandy-legged coon cat that had adopted her, and maybe Steven Schwinger, that sideways-walking hound well past his prime. Every now and then, Cleo would be loping alongside her. Then the book would be put away, and the two girls would yak it up as if they might run out of time while they still had so much to say to each other. To other people, Katie never said much about Cleo, except to repeat ordinary bits of common folklore she attributed to her friend's unique wisdom.

*Cleo says*, she might remark at dinner, *that soap is a kind of magnet. It pulls dirt right from the skin.*

Or, *Cleo says a howling dog on a still night means that someone is dying.*

Or, *Cleo says if you press an ice cube against a wood sliver stuck in your finger, it will poke itself out, and you can pull it free, just like that.*

By the end of Katie's first year with her aunt and uncle, the Schwingers couldn't imagine how they'd lived without her—or without Cleo, either. The older girl liked to help Katie's elderly uncle with heavy

< 81 >

work, stacking wood and forking over the rocky garden soil. She even learned a complicated bit of wiring from Katie, who seemingly could pick up anything from a library book. Together, the two girls redid the Schwingers' frayed and overloaded electrical box. The old couple fell in love with Cleo despite themselves, and soon, like Katie, they drifted away when the conversation downtown turned to shattered birdbaths or missing cigarettes or girl-sized footprints razing a tulip bed.

---

The friendship went on like this for a couple of years until the November Cleo turned fifteen; Katie, an awkward thirteen-year-old. Overnight, their worlds divided as Cleo transformed and conceived other, more pressing, interests. She was still notoriously unkempt: her pretty hair, streaked with gold, always tangled; her clothes held together with bent safety pins; her nails...well...please. Yet, remarkably, she was a beauty, and the smell of her—musky and faintly sweet—flat-out enticed. That effect was not lost on Cleo. As she moved through her teenage years, she discovered a new way to terrorize town. One year passed, another, and she discovered she could scare the pants, literally, off any man she chose. Her promiscuity was legendary: the city meter reader, Hanson; the young baker, Donadio; that jaunty shipwright; a third-grade teacher; the Czech plumber; the new doctor with the pregnant wife. That last one nearly stopped her cold. The wife went after her with an antique gun from the doctor's collection, which fortunately for everyone had been poorly assembled and fell into three pieces before it could be used. There was talk of involving Kane. Surely, he'd step in to protect the girl from herself. But by the time anyone thought to rouse her grandfather, Cleo was closing in on her eighteenth birthday, becoming what her grandfather liked to call "an independent gal." She hadn't so much as talked to her own parents in months. And, in the end, she'd easily released the young

< 82 >

doctor, moving on to a fellow at the beer distributorship, then to one of her old playmates, a Knutson, who never would get over her.

All this time, Katie went on about her own business. It was as if she and Cleo had had a talk and recognized that both had tasks ahead of them that required a temporary separation. Without Cleo around, Katie was alone more, but she didn't really seem to mind. She was winning awards in high school for her math and science, and people were starting to talk about her as if she might put the town on a map someday. She was that smart. Her aunt said Katie dreamed of being a veterinarian and even confided in one of the library ladies that she and the uncle were thinking of cashing in some bonds they'd bought decades ago. The Schwingers had been seen talking to Harry Kane, too, about a piece of land he'd long wanted to buy from them. An education like the one Katie deserved wasn't going to come cheaply. Katie wasn't ignorant of the expenses ahead either. She had a dozen projects in the works—a fruit stand, a summer pet-sitting business—and one of her math teachers finagled a part-time job for Katie, filing for an accountant. Yet somehow, she managed each day to get back up Quarry Road in the cool late afternoon to take old Steven Schwinger, the hound, out for a little meandering, stopping now and then in the middle of the empty, dusty lane to fill a collapsible bowl with water from an old soda bottle and wait while the old dog took a few grateful laps.

Sometimes, out of nowhere, Cleo would appear, and the two would walk awhile like old times, oblivious to the world around them. Katie's aunt said later that was probably part of the charm of the walks for Katie—the chance that Cleo might appear.

"Katie never judged that girl," the aunt said. "And wouldn't let anyone else either. 'Cleo's on a mission,' Katie would tell us, dead serious, as if Cleo was engaged in something more than teenage catting around, bless her soul."

And yet Cleo might have gone on indefinitely, working her way through town with a parade of one-night stands, romantic weeks, a giddy month, a missing weekend—one near-violent surge after another—save for Davis Riddell.

---

He arrived on a boat, the way most trouble did in town. A trimaran way too big and grand to escape notice, all varnished teak and gleaming lines. At first, they thought he might be some kind of celebrity, but no one recognized him, and he wasn't exactly hiding away. He drank with the others down at the Courthouse Tavern and was friendly enough, showing reticence only when a couple of the older Finns hinted they might like to come aboard his boat. Then the rumors began to shift: he was a drug runner, moving pot from British Columbia into the States, exchanging it for harder stuff he'd transport back up through the Gulf Islands to Johnstone Strait, all the way up to some hidey hole in the back of beyond. No one paid much attention to pleasure sailboats up there. You could anchor in a jeweled bay and rendezvous with anything: a motor boat, a float plane, a kayak, for crissakes.

"Well, what's he up to here then, I wonder?" my brother Ed said, innocently.

"No good, I'd bet," Curtis Schwinger answered from down the bar, his dull eagerness nearly killing the discussion.

"Nah," one of Kane's men said after a moment. "If he's a drug-runner, I'd say he's on vacation. Fellow's the most relaxed criminal I've ever seen—always taking a walk or a bike ride, sipping coffee half the day at the café."

"You guys don't have a clue, do you?" Curtis Schwinger said. He'd grown a little quieter over the years, but once he got a tirade going, it was clear to all his conspiracy theories had only become more entrenched, more terrified, meaner. That day his face was flushed, and his right hand tapped erratically on the bartop.

"You should spend a day or two up at the courthouse," he spat out. "See the Meth-Head Parade arrive from out in the county, all spindle-jerky and bug-eyed, thieving eyes scanning the corridors, even with a cop right next to them, leading them by the wrists."

"But we're not in the county. We're in town," Ed countered.

"Spitting on the floors, pocketing anything not bolted to the ground, dragging along their scrummy kids, who, you know, are going to end up just like them, driving..."

"Kids driving cars? Holy crap, what will the world come to?" one of the Finns interrupted with a straight face.

"I spied that fellow the other night from my window," Curtis Schwinger said, leaning closer. "Three in the morning. Who's out wandering around at three in the morning?"

There was a long pause along the bar as everyone considered, then another of Kane's men, my brother's friend Tork said, "You 'spied' him? You 'spied' him? God, you're such an old woman, Schwinger. Who's peering through his curtains at three in the morning?"

---

No one knows for sure how they truly met. Cleo might have been practicing her handstands one windy night, almost floating up and down the rocking boat dock, when Davis Riddell returned from one of his own late night rambles. He might have seen her from a distance, dimly illuminated in the single light, and might have done what no one had ever been able: sneak up on Cleo Talmadge. Or maybe he witnessed one of her vaults over a brambly garden hedge, another old skill and an old habit, too, since her hands would most likely have been clutching "something interesting." Or perhaps, on an empty, moonlit sidewalk, the world asleep around them, their solitary paths simply collided.

My brother Ed was visiting the tavern, one of the last to call it quits one night, when Cleo and Davis Riddell wandered in together. The expression on Cleo's face was so uncharacteristic, he didn't recognize her at first. Gone was the private grin, the tilted chin, the half-closed eyes that despite the appearance of languor seemed to take in every little thing. The Cleo beside Davis Riddell had a washed-clean openness, an unfamiliar vulnerability that made the bartender grimace until he too recognized her and released an involuntary guffaw.

"Your usual, Cleo," he murmured as he turned to fill a highball glass with Coke and an illicit splash of rum. "You'll have to make it quick."

"Just want to get a six-pack from you—that Alaskan, if you've got it, " Davis Riddell said. He held a twenty in his left hand, and for the first time, Ed noticed the man's right hand tightly grasped Cleo's.

The bartender nodded and went to a side cooler and pulled out the beer, slipped it into a paper sack, and set it on the bar. While the bartender made change, Ed caught Davis Riddell's eye.

"She's barely legal, you know," he said, not unkindly.

The bartender turned to hand over a few bills, hanging onto them just a second longer than necessary.

"And a whole world of trouble, too," he added.

Davis Riddell smiled as he pocketed his change and picked up the paper sack.

"I'll take my chances," he said.

It was only after they left that Ed and the bartender realized that Cleo hadn't spit out a word. Nor had she even looked at them. Her attention was entirely claimed by Riddell. They had to share that with the others the next night. It was a bit of news—the drug runner taking up with Cleo—and it hit them all. A wave of yearning swept across the tavern, the youngest Knutson, the lovesick one, flailing hardest in its wake.

Davis Riddell was thirty-one to her eighteen. Not a handsome

< 86 >

man, not really, but well-worn: muscular and easy all at once. He must have been capable, sailing that big boat all by himself, but he was an odd sort, too. He never seemed to sleep, for one thing. Until he found Cleo, he was spotted all over town, scribbling on scraps of paper as if he were mapping the place. Then again, a lot of sailors can't escape scrutiny when they arrive in town. We watch them find their land legs and make the constant trek from the boat haven up Bay Road into town. There's no buses here, so if you want to get around, you either walk or hitch a ride. It's a hard place to hide—until you get out closer to the county line, out past Quarry Road, for instance.

Cleo must have taken him there. How else would he have found his way out to the Schwingers'? And he must have, because late one Friday, there was Davis Riddell sitting at the bar in the Courthouse Tavern, having a quick beer before he met Cleo. On the bar in front of him he'd set down an old tomato juice can, a brand no longer available for sale, piled high with a type of golden raspberry Curtis Schwinger recognized as his mother's own hybrid. She made a golden jam that won ribbons every year at the county fair. Some words apparently passed between Curtis and Davis Riddell. The bartender overheard their conversation only as a distant murmur; he was hoisting a case of beer on his shoulder, creaking up the cellar steps. When later, he recalled their raised voices, he declared it must have been Curtis, raving again, lost in one of his mad rants. It being a Friday, an early court day, Curtis had been in the tavern since four, and none of Kane's men had arrived yet to temper Davis Riddell's cryptic answer, his cocky grin—to put it all into proper perspective. Ten minutes later, after Davis Riddell had downed his beer and departed, Curtis telephoned a courthouse coworker, but he couldn't help at all, of course. There's no law, the fellow reminded Curtis, against sharing produce, regardless of the container.

It was just the following Sunday evening when the Schwingers began calling around, looking for Katie. She'd gone off for her walk with Steven Schwinger in the late morning, and by mid-afternoon, she still hadn't returned. Alf Schwinger, the old uncle, found the half-blind hound stuck on a stone ledge on the town side of the Knutson place, howling into a bush as if he expected it to uproot itself and help him home. The uncle wondered if perhaps Katie actually had brought the dog home before heading toward town to pursue one of her latest money-making endeavors and the old, confused hound had followed. But it was Sunday, and Katie would have noticed Steven Schwinger behind her, and not one bit of this seemed right. By suppertime, with no sign of Katie, the Schwingers were seriously worried.

They telephoned Alicia and Tim Talmadge, disturbing a quiet Sunday supper of poached eggs and toast points. Cleo was staying with her grandfather, the Schwingers were told. No, neither Alicia nor Tim had seen her that day. They'd been painting the spare room, uh, Cleo's room actually.

Harry Kane didn't know where Cleo was either, but my brother Ed was in the Kane's side yard, flipping hamburgers for the Sunday barbecue, and he weighed in.

"Try the tavern," he suggested, helpfully pointing out that Davis Riddell was a frequent visitor there.

And so the old uncle, Alf Schwinger, took off in the failing light once more, while his wife tended to a still-distraught Steven Schwinger, who would not quit howling in the dust of the driveway and would not come inside the house either.

From his regular corner, Curtis Schwinger saw his father enter the Courthouse Tavern and go straight to the bar, the question already on his lips, and disheveled as he was, Curtis managed to slip down

< 88 >

the hallway towards the men's room and out the back door beside the basement steps. Curtis did not get on well with his folks these days. In fact, on Friday, after his futile call to his courthouse friend, Curtis had apparently driven out to his parents' place and threatened to put them in a home. His mother, shaken, had confided in her pastor just that morning. It had been such a shock to the old couple, that tirade. And now this—Katie's disappearance.

Alf Schwinger stepped right aboard Davis Riddell's boat and knocked on the hatch, which was partially open. It was past nine by then, a summer dusk, and although a thin line of light still lit the mountains behind the bay, night was clearly upon them. Still, Cleo's boyfriend had a gas lantern burning on the galley shelf, and so Alf eased up the half-open hatch and called out again. Almost at once, he saw, sitting next to the lantern, one of his wife's old tomato juice cans, the one she sent Davis home with just a few days ago when he and Cleo stopped by with a chinook Cleo said she'd caught herself. It was so quiet that for a moment Alf was certain no one was about. Then he realized that what he'd taken at first for a bundle of laundry balanced on the bunk's edge was the fellow's stocking feet lying, twisted, over the bunk's edge. It didn't take more than another step forward for Alf to see the rest of it, and all the time his old heart was hammering: *Where's Katie?*

---

They found them just before midnight, the moonlight streaming a path that led straight to them. *Two girls off Quarry Road*, the police scanner reported. Two girls lying almost in plain sight, nearly holding hands. A heart, a head, a full-on execution. The love-struck Knutson, an early volunteer, discovered them. The other Finns had to pull him away. He was raging so much they feared he'd kill someone himself.

At first, the theory was that one of Davis Riddell's drug buddies had tracked him down and that somehow Cleo and Katie had borne witness to their reunion. Plausible, even likely, except it turned out Davis Riddell hadn't been a drug runner at all, but a burnt-out musician with a trust fund, allergic to every possible drug, couldn't even take one for his insomnia.

It was Harry Kane who figured out the truth. It turned out he'd been listening all the while to the tavern stories, repeated each morning in one rumbling truck cab after another, and he might have ended up in jail himself if my brother Ed hadn't intervened and got the police to Curtis Schwinger's right on Harry Kane's heels. Who even knew the old fellow could still move that fast? He had Curtis's throat in one hand almost as soon as he slammed across the threshold.

"Jealous of a little girl," Harry Kane swore. "You son of a bitch."

It was bad blood, everyone agreed. It showed up in all kinds of families, even those with kind, well-meaning parents like the Schwingers. Those poor sad people with all that bad blood running through the family. Ed told me Curtis had a cousin did the same thing, killed his girlfriend and would have gotten to his own little daughter too if he weren't so high he hadn't forgotten where he left his trailer. She got away that time.

< 90 >

# PINK CLOUD

The first time he took her to his house the sunset was the excuse. A perfunctory invitation, since neither of them had any real desire for a relationship. Everyday encounters still seemed too fragile to allow for that kind of faith and potential messiness. That's not what they yearned for—no, not at all. Still, each had a lot to make up for in their respective circles, and they tried to please or at least appear to do so. So, here they were, set up by friends, privately dismissing at first glance, without disappointment, any possibility of romance.

No chemistry, she decided.

Not his type, he concluded.

Perhaps it was this, then, the mutual release of those expectations, that allowed them to relax at the restaurant their kind friends had chosen for them. A Christian family of teetotalers ran the place. They catered to clientele who could claim tentative triumph here, unimpeded by temptations. The two ate with pleasure, a rich meal a joy still permitted them, and laughed together at their own gluttony. As they threw their napkins down, Tucker asked if she wanted to see his view.

"It's stunning," he promised. "Really, my family paid good money for that vista. My mother believes it will sustain me."

"You're lucky," she told him. "My brother bought me a dog."

"*Watch*dog," he nodded. "They got me one of those, too."

He did not offer her a glass of wine at his house, and she did not expect one. Their mutual recoveries were certainly a condition of their date, the gold-rimmed fact that made their friends think, *Ah, they*

< 91 >

*have so much in common.* A sunset was in progress, and before they reclined on his couch and watched the wall of windows glow pink, he ground coffee beans and boiled water and, mug in hand, pointed out landmarks as they appeared against the darkening sky: high-rises outlined in lights, a steeple, the famous tower glowing gold. His dog, a terrier-mutt who'd been officially registered as a service dog for his emotional needs, wandered into the living room and clambered onto the couch beside them with all the lumbering grace of a woman in a bathrobe. She eased her head down into his lap awkwardly as if trying on sincerity.

"I never had pets before Trish here," he said, scratching the dog's tense ears.

"Mine is a Lab," she said. "It's like having a mother in the house. If I'm in the kitchen too long, she eyeballs me. If I lock the bathroom door, she hovers outside, breathing heavily. Linger and she sticks her paw beneath the door and rattles it. I think Ben must have gone to one of those rescue dog camps where they train the dogs to drag out bodies. She hauls me from bed if I oversleep. They must have implanted a timer in her."

"And if you don't get up?" he asked.

For a long moment, the question lingered unanswered in the air between them.

*This world is not enough,* one note declared, its author having chosen to travel on to what he most assuredly assumed was a richer, deeper, sky-driven world, the kind of place that won't wait for you to rise on you own hind legs and become a man, but swoops in and grabs you and throws you pell-mell into *real* life—rejoicing, full-bodied *life.*

*This world is too much,* another note wept, her hand too weak to hold the pencil, which in any case, was not well-sharpened, a nub of a thing barely able to make an imprint on the broad clean swath of white paper, not unlike her mark in this life. She slipped away, that effort the first

< 92 >

she'd mastered. In her new world, life will be a pleasant pea, a round diminutive thing she can swallow easily without worry of indigestion.

"Good point," she pretended to consider. "It's not as if the dog can dial the phone."

He nodded—they were in perfect agreement—and offered her a pink marshmallow cookie from a cellophane package. As the cookie passed between them, his dog sniffed the broken air. They laughed despite themselves, a shared and prolonged laugh, an improbability that astonished them. It was nice, sitting there on his couch with the heat of the dog pressing against their thighs, real smiles playing on their lips. So nice. The moment couldn't help but remind them of others.

"I have...," he began.

Was there something in his voice, the way his eyes flicked toward a kitchen cupboard? The dog must have seen it as well. A low growl held them in place, while outside slips of pink cloud drifted by and the sky began to darken as the night they'd been awaiting finally arrived.

# MY WITNESS

In the back booth at Castonova's Grill, my sister positions a photograph on the table between us. Her speech is over, but her cheeks are pink from the effort of getting the words right. She's been trying to tell me for weeks, she insists. I already knew. Hell, everyone knew. Right and left I've been glad-handed, the big brother continually congratulated on his sister's good fortune. Still, I pretend her news has not yet reached my ears. My hand bypasses the photograph, reaching for my wine glass instead. Not so old Bella, who manages to slide our hot plates before us—sausage and peppers for me, spinach ravioli for Ellen—and commandeer the photograph in one swift movement. She pinches the photo with two fingers and holds it up for scrutiny.

"So this is the guy, the fiancé," she says, fisting her potholders on one hip while she squints at the photograph in her other hand. "Your billionaire."

"We grew up together, Bella," Ellen says. "Don't you remember the O'Sheas?"

Bella shakes her head. "I remember the Sullivans. The McMenamins. I remember that priest, McGuire."

"Seven boys," Ellen prods. "On Constance Avenue."

"You know this guy?" Bella asks me.

I reluctantly glance at the photograph of Michael O'Shea, Ellen enclosed in his arms. I consider the man's receding hairline and muscular forearms. The cuteness of the pose: his face thrust forward, cheek to cheek with Ellen's. He looks like no one I have ever known, no one, in fact, I ever want to know.

< 94 >

Bella snorts, pokes a finger at the photograph. "Look at that expression. That's one satisfied fellow, in't he? The cat who swallowed the canary." She puts the photograph back before Ellen, but keeps her head inclined toward it as if wondering whether she's missing something.

"Would that make you the canary?" I ask Ellen.

Bella swats me on the shoulder with her potholders.

"*You*," she grunts. "And when am I gonna get an invitation to your wedding? How 'bout you and that Teresa, huh? That shut him up, didn't it?" she laughs, bobbing her head towards Ellen.

Bella stretches her pudgy hand across my plate for the carafe of wine she'd left on the table earlier and tops off each of our glasses, making sure I get the lion's share. I forgive her instantly.

"Enjoy," she commands as she shuffles off.

"What's this about Teresa Livitz?" Ellen asks, smiling, as I occupy myself with dinner.

I can't answer her, of course. A piece of sausage will not stay on my fork. I have to chase it around my plate.

"Laurie?" Ellen says again. Then, more sharply: "Lawrence?" Her ravioli remains untouched, the spinach glowing through the thin egg noodles. "He'll be here in less than a month, Laurie."

The wine glass jerks a little in my hand. "My good buddy," I mutter into the glass, then swallow hard, as if I've just given a toast.

Of course I'm talking about Teresa Livitz, a woman who vows she will not be listed in my obituary as my "dear companion." "Call me 'Buddy' one more time," she swore to me over the phone last week, "and I will not be responsible for my actions." Teresa, patient and enduring. The definition of a buddy in my book. Still, I guess Ellen could be forgiven for believing that by "buddy" I meant her own fiancé, the fabulous Michael O'Shea.

< 95 >

From second grade through our last year of junior high school, it had been O'Shea who played the role of my best friend. During much of that same time, unbeknownst to me, Michael and Ellen nurtured a mutual childish attraction for each other. Nothing came of it then, of course. Ellen was nearly two years younger, a whole generation at that age. The O'Sheas moved to Rhode Island. I eventually surrendered to college; our parents went down like dominos; Ellen married badly. Who could keep in touch? Who wanted to? Then last year, the Rec Department went online, and Ellen, the social services director, became the last woman alive to plunge into the world of the Internet. I would have thought my sister would go mad for the multitudes of blogs and forums, but Ellen was oddly reticent when it came to online discussions. What she did like was Facebook. She plugged in every name she could think of from our childhood: neighbors, distant cousins, old teachers, our father's old coworkers, even the policeman who came when our Uncle Satch fell off the roof one drunken Fourth of July, a nosy cop who snooped around like a rogue detective, hungry for a case. For a while she had this idea of making her research a project called *Where Are They Now? A Saga of Personal History*.

Her sojourn through Facebook was eerily efficient, although she never friended a single soul. She simply traveled through the ether, through time and space, and began collecting on her own. Ever old school, Ellen cleared a wall in her apartment, tacked up a map, and began to litter the wall with index cards and addresses. She found O'Shea in Bend, Oregon, and, on impulse, did what she hadn't managed to do with anyone else: she emailed him. Of course he remembered her. I gulp from my wine glass and picture the Michael O'Shea of my sister's photograph, whipping from one high-powered email to another, when Ellen's missive arrived like a rogue cell of pre-teen longing finally locating its target.

The whole enterprise is one that, frankly, I would prefer not to think about. And until recently I've been nimbly evasive, distracting not just the plans aimed on a coming reunion, but the announcement of the wedding itself. Yet, once her news is delivered, Ellen's focus is unrelenting. A countdown of days begins, leading up to O'Shea's arrival, and my sister transforms into the pest of my youth, badgering me with daily phone calls. Michael, she keeps saying, is anxious to see me.

"I have a life too, you know, Ellen," I tell her. I imply that I'm too busy teaching my one remedial science class at Bishop Wood High School's summer school, too busy caring for a statue-like iguana belonging to Teresa Livitz's son, Stanny, too busy to drop everything for O'Shea.

"Saturday, then," Ellen says firmly.

She's got me now, and we both know it. My routine on Saturday mornings is set. I must attend my weekly meditation class, followed by a swim at the Rec Center. After that, without fail, I meet Ellen for a late breakfast at her condo.

"Okay," I tell her. "Okay, okay. I'll meet him, but after...after brunch."

"Thank you," Ellen says with only a trace of relief in her voice.

---

Each of the other eight people in my meditation class seems to visualize a personal sanctuary easily, but for weeks now, I've failed to conjure up what my meditation instructor, Ula, calls my "home spot." I tried a basketball court first, but immediately imagined a group of anvil-headed thugs who invaded and stole my ball. Next, I conjured an elegant city apartment with an amiable doorman who allowed only me to enter the building. This worked for a full three minutes until the doorman inexplicably turned psychotic, acquiring a police dog who chased me into an elevator with no interior buttons. No matter

< 97 >

how hard I try to keep things even and pleasant, there's a tiny but vocal doom-saying part of my consciousness that won't let my boat float—so to speak. *What if*, that little Lawrence seems to say, *what if some nut with a machete suddenly arrives?* And then all of sudden what do I see in whatever visualization of nirvana I've conjured but a crazy-eyed, knife-wielding intruder. God help me.

Ula tells me that I shouldn't be fearful of these intrusions, that they represent my own conflict about undertaking a new route of self-discovery.

"You've got to inhabit *that* realm, Lawrence. You must give testimony to its existence," she says. "Otherwise, you see, you're not really in *this* world."

My home spot, according to Ula, is the key, the Rosetta Stone, to all the issues in my life, and only by occupying my home spot fully and allowing a life to unfold in that nether region will I be able to make sense of my life. This is a theory to which Teresa Livitz, the secretary at Bishop Wood High School (and Ula's baby sister), also subscribes. It was Teresa—now vacationing fiercely at a lake in northern Minnesota with her two children and her dead husband's parents—who arranged my presence in Ula's home. It is part of her attempt—*our* attempt—to make sense of our relationship. I conceded easily. I've always appreciated Ula's sonorous voice, and I actually enjoy the hours I spend in her basement meditation room, everyone lined up in green plastic lawn chairs against the two concrete block walls, all of us pretending we aren't there. This collective disappearing act cracked me up at first, but now I've come to think of meditation as a form of prayer: prayer with pictures. Still, I'm not yet willing to leave behind the role of the supplicant for that of a tiny personal god. Time after time, I have fled whole worlds of my own creation as faceless, unnamable revelations nipped at my heels.

But this Saturday morning, a surprise: When I close my eyes and

< 98 >

"go into the center of my head," a lighthouse appears. It seems familiar somehow, and I relax, allowing it to substantiate in my mind's eye. Have I been here? Of course I haven't. I have never been out of Ohio, have never even driven up to the Great Lakes. I can't remember seeing a single lighthouse in person, and yet here one is, replicated in loving detail by my surprising unconscious. Occupying a tiny spit of land jutting off a smooth, untrammeled beach, the lighthouse is a picture postcard of isolation, nary a pirate ship nor devastating storm in sight. Only the slightest of inner breezes hints at my waking anxiety, the imminent discord of my inevitable meeting with Michael O'Shea.

As my lighthouse's beacon sweeps over deserted waters, I feel myself crack open in a way that I can't define, and I hope to hell I won't cry the way half the rest of the class has, snuffling over Ula's Kleenex box when the Big Revelation finally hits home. Somehow I manage to get out of Ula's basement with my dignity intact. Even so, my Saturday swim at the Rec is also cut short by an abrupt wave of sentimentality that hits me as I watch a pair of boys goading each other into greater and greater feats off the high dive, and an hour later, as I let myself into Ellen's condominium, that old ache rises again in my chest. I'm almost relieved when my sister appears and frowns as usual over my wet hair and wrinkled fingers, my khaki shorts, twisted and slightly damp in the seat.

"You've been to the pool," she says, flatly.

I nod and lumber past her toward the living room where she has laid out plates stacked with slices of coffeecake and pre-buttered bagels as if I am a visitor too impaired to trust with a knife. Her own hands tense at her sides as I pluck out a bagel and settle myself on the couch.

"A meditation class followed by all that physical tumult—doesn't the latter negate the former?"

"Quite the opposite," I say. "That kind of noise is very cleansing, actually. Clean white noise."

< 99 >

"Like that dream you used to have," Ellen muses.

Dream? I examine Ellen closely, wondering if today will be the day I'll find signs of encroaching dementia. All of the older relatives on our mother's side of the family have given way to early senility, the first signs of which were a recounting of a false past.

"Remember those horses," our grandmother had begun. "The Appaloosa was my own, my sweet Ginger." Day by day, she had recounted bits and pieces of a ranch childhood—she, who had been born and raised in Philadelphia, daughter of a pharmacist—until finally her fantasy life was all she could remember: the big breakfasts, the fence-mending, the two-day treks to retrieve stock. At her last Thanksgiving, the smell of the sage-sausage stuffing sent her into a trance, mumbling about the Canadian prairie.

With Uncle Shelby, the World War II pacifist, memory had come in the form of a dream stint as a fighter pilot, and another relative, a great-aunt, had spent years mooning over a continually expanding collection of photographs depicting West Highland Whites, a breed of terriers she claimed to have discovered while vacationing in York nearly a century before.

"I don't dream," I say, rehashing a long-ago argument. "Remember, I don't have a talent for dreaming."

"Oh, Laurie," Ellen sighs, "you make no sense. How can someone who can't dream meditate?" She shakes her head slowly, still musing. "Must have been William then. He used to dream that he was trapped beneath a shifting column of slowly falling salt. A terrifying dream, you'd think. *He* found it refreshing. No wonder I left him."

William Underwood, Ellen's first husband. A man I never stopped thinking of as "that Unitarian." After six years of vicious calm, he'd left Ellen, running off with a girl from his Youth in Transition committee.

"Ellen," I begin, making my voice soft and warning.

"Oh, shoot, Laurie, I know who did the leaving. Don't think I'm rewriting the past. Well, maybe I am—a little—but not on purpose. Really, I'm getting stupid with these wedding plans. Who gets married at forty-seven? Why is that?" Ellen stops for a moment in her bustling to stare hard at me. "I mean, why do you think, Laurie, that we have this push to get married after all?"

"*I* don't," I say, picking up a large piece of coffee cake. As I do, I am almost positive I hear a phantom Teresa Livitz click her tongue in exasperation.

My sister shoves a plate under my hands, barely catching several large crumbs.

"It's not loneliness. I'm not lonely, you know. I wonder if it's ownership," she continues. "Or maybe we get married to have a witness, someone to verify that we've really been here. I've thought long and hard about this, you know, Laurie. I don't *need* to get married."

She pauses, waiting for me to chime in with reassurances or questions. I pour myself a mug of coffee instead. Ellen tucks herself into an armchair and continues as if I've actually responded.

"Our parents, you know, their marriage was no model, but then it wasn't a bad marriage either. And Michael and I—well, we've both made mistakes."

I pick at the topping of my coffee cake, eating the cherries one at a time and trying to override my sister's voice by fabricating a surging lap of waves against my lighthouse beach. It's no good. I've been in the apartment less than ten minutes, and already I've lost my grip. When I close my eyes, the windows of my lighthouse film with fog. The beacon flickers and dims. Now all I can see is the stranger, Michael O'Shea, challenging me from Ellen's photograph. O'Shea's unfamiliar white-toothed grin proclaiming his success in all things. Because this is another thing, this business about O'Shea's huge success. He's made millions apparently, selling books. One of his company's catalogs filled with self-described "tomes of emancipation" taunts me from Ellen's coffee table.

Revenge books? I've read about books like those, books with titles like *How to Grow Your Own Money*, or *An Insider's Guide to Ripping Off the Vatican*, or *Take Back the Block: Sixty Ways to Put Your Neighbors in the Hospital*.

"They're just how-to books, Laurie," Ellen says, following my gaze. "Modern day homesteading—provisions, tool-making—that sort of thing. Michael specializes in survival."

I reach for another piece of cake.

"You're always hungry. You've noticed that, haven't you?" Ellen says, not unkindly, but poking for a reaction. "I mean, always eating. Who knows if you're hungry. Are you hungry, Laurie?"

"I'm not the one who has to fit into a wedding dress."

"Speaking of which," Ellen continues, "Michael is expecting us. He can't wait to see you, you know. And he's had another idea for the wedding ceremony."

"No speeches, " I say, wiping my hands on one of the napkins Ellen offers. "And I will not join hands in a circle."

"We'll take my car," my sister says, ignoring me as she grabs her purse. "Your seats are probably damp."

———

For the wedding and his triumphant return, O'Shea has taken on a house on the town hill, Saint's Ridge. The mountain, they call it in town. He's staying *on the mountain* in one of the new, sprawling, multi-level mansions built beside Lord's Lake, smack on the former property of the Catholic retreat house. I wonder if O'Shea has done this on purpose, if he remembers our last shared summer before the O'Sheas vanished into Rhode Island.

St. Anthony's is gone now, torn down to make room for Saint's

Ridge Estates. St. Anthony, Finder of Lost Objects. As a kid, I always
thought it was funny and faintly cruel that they'd named the retreat
house—home to the infirm and senile nuns, so many lost objects
themselves—after that particular saint. Now it seems just right.

The passenger seat of Ellen's old Corolla is missing some of its
stuffing, and I sit much lower than my sister. My head is barely on
level with her shoulder. We drive down South Fort Street, turn onto
Pleasant Avenue, glide past Ula's pink brick home. I spot Ula's purple
straw hat bobbing between the shrubs and shrink a bit further in my
seat the way I imagine my own students—the dilatory ones—do when
they see me coming. With my hands folded, hair slicked back, I've
become a little boy, the idiot brother left in my younger sister's care.

O'Shea and I had a terrible time ditching Ellen that summer. We
chased her for blocks, pelting her with pine cones. We took the wheels
off her bike and hid them under a tarp in O'Shea's garage. Yet no
matter how much I threatened her, how often I sabotaged her, she
persistently appeared behind us, sometimes blocks and blocks away,
a tiny pony-tailed speck, pedaling unerringly in our direction. I glance
over at her now. Her hair, still soft and long and brown, is held off her
face by a silver barrette. *She's* hardly changed, I think. I close my eyes,
surprised at how much I long for the serenity of the lighthouse, but
it's O'Shea, not the home spot, I see: O'Shea, the crew-cutted, thin-
lipped boy, wearing blue jeans and a gray Bishop Wood sweatshirt, its
sleeves cut off at the elbows.

We'd been just shy of thirteen, both of our birthdays coming up
that last August. To get to Lord's Lake, we had to pass through the
retreat forest, a dense, moldy woods with too much history. During
the Revolutionary War, the bodies of deserters and spies had hung from
the winter-bare limbs as warnings to other wayward boys scavenging
too far from camp in their soldier rags. Even in my own childhood, the
woods and the lake path were rumored to be haunted by a nun who

had disappeared from the retreat house an eon ago. Dogs had come upon a bit of disturbed earth, hollowed like an empty almost-grave; an odd light, a sort of will-o'-the-wisp, had been reported by hunters who frequented the woods in autumn; and even we once found a cache of water-stained garments in a hollow by the lake shore along with a pair of black shoes, the laces missing.

Equally unnerving was the stretch of road bordered by busts of long-forgotten Catholic martyrs. A quarter mile up the steep narrow road, shrouded by trees, suddenly curved sharply and flattened, and out of nowhere, the heads appeared on both sides. Set on concrete pedestals, pitted and chipped by their exposure to dozens of winter cold snaps, the busts never failed to jar me. Lacking the distraction of bodies, the heads seemed to focus on me as if they could see me more clearly than anyone ever had. All my boyish flaws—my greed, my growing lust and ease at lying—appeared clearly before me then like a shadow over my real everyday self. That stretch of the avenue scared me more than I would ever admit and often set my mind wandering into morbid scenarios wherein I would be punished for my sins. I hated lingering by the heads, but often we did just that, waiting for Ellen, whose squeaking bicycle chain O'Shea swore he could hear approaching.

The lake was the draw. As if magnetized, we'd found our way to the decrepit boathouse and a long wooden skiff, rotting under a tattered and moldy blue tarp. We would bicycle up the lonely road, our army surplus backpacks and wire bike baskets filled to the brim with pilfered tools and tins of sealant. I was the schemer, the one with all the plans, but O'Shea, it turned out, had a talent for stealing and an old senile uncle whose garage was never locked. We spent days working together, bare-chested in the sunny clearing where we'd dragged "our" boat, readying it for the morning we'd launch it into the lake. As we worked, I cast my eyes over the woods from time to time. To stave off my own terror, I would test my fears out on Michael as if they were theories, events we could prepare for and prevent.

"What if," I'd say, "a madman escaped from a prison hospital and found his way to these woods?"

"What if he's got his eye on this boat?"

"What if he is watching us now right now, waiting for a chance to pick off one of us?"

Michael would always deflect each possibility. "Naw," he'd say, his grin reassuring me. "Couldn't happen."

Picturing us there on that forgotten graveled shore, just the two of us, I release a shuddering sigh that encourages Ellen to nudge me roughly just as the road, much wider now and curving in a way I don't remember, emerges from the trees.

"Laurie, wake up, now," she says. "We're nearly there."

---

At about the same spot where I reckon the line of heads should appear, Ellen slows at a security checkpoint complete with surveillance cameras. The uniformed guard, a pale, bug-eyed man in his mid-thirties, recognizes her car and waves us through, although not before managing to duck his head and scrutinize me, trussed up in the old Corolla's twisted, fraying seat belt. The expression on the man's face is no doubt meant to be stern and forbidding, but I think he looks shockingly simple.

"A Kilpatrick—Raymee Kilpatrick," Ellen says, after we pass. "Remember, the son who won't move out. His parents are thrilled he's working at last. Michael hired him for the wedding, too."

"You need security for the wedding?"

My sister gives me a curious look. "Parking, Laurie."

What an odd transformation, I think, as we travel past one ridiculously large tract home after another. Snatches of the woods remain, just enough to hint at what has been stolen. The developers have smoothed out the open wildness of the woods and sewn it into pockets, making it civilized, yet somehow even more secret.

———————

Over the years my students have returned to visit me without their hair, with low-slung beer bellies or tattoos, smudged pouches under their eyes. Memory is not my problem; I always recognize the long-missing, the near-forgotten. Still, I am taken aback when, after untangling myself from the Corolla's seat belts, I stumble onto a brick driveway straight into a stranger's embrace.

"Laurie," the man exclaims, his hands clutching my forearms. "My god, can this really be you? You've grown!"

Young Michael O'Shea had been shyly diffident, a remarkably contained child who had fashioned a whole vocabulary out of a shrug. This man effuses. He engulfs me in another hug, a tight, intimate hug, his shaking hands tickling my waist.

"I was beginning to wonder if you'd ever make it up here, Laurie," he says. When he abruptly releases his hold, I notice the man's eyes are damp. His grin—those white, white teeth—looks painful. "C'mon, Laurie, let me show you this place."

As the three of us tour the ridiculous home, wandering past the rented furnishings and the deceptively paneled kitchen with its granite counters and cowed, faintly surly maids, the unease that began in the driveway coalesces into certainty.

*No way*, I think. There's no way this man could be our Michael O'Shea.

First: the thin skin and delicate complexion, often suffused with pink, that typified the O'Sheas as I remembered them, is missing from this grown—should I say "half-grown"—Michael. Because despite his muscular forearms, this leathery O'Shea is much too short and thin. He's almost a midget. Ellen, a scrap of a woman, hovers nearly a half-inch above this O'Shea. My Michael O'Shea towered over me in the seventh grade and wore pants one size larger.

*What does this man want with my sister?* I wonder. *With me?*

I pull back and allow this fiancé to steer Ellen through a bank of French doors onto a verandah of flawless Pennsylvania blue slate. For a moment, the beauty of this pretend paradise knocks my fears to one side as I squint to take in the oversize urns trailing ivy and geraniums, the perfect pool below, the lake beyond. Water burbles. The fragrance of fresh mown grass wafts. Under an umbrella, on a glass-topped table, a large yellow bowl is filled with fresh strawberries on ice. Beside it, a rose-colored china plate piled with crustless sandwiches, a bottle of chilled white wine sweating in the heat.

Ellen groans at the sight of the food.

"Oh, Michael, I told you we would be eating at my place."

He shrugs cheerfully as if to say, I couldn't help myself, honey. He eases out a chair for Ellen, his hand briefly lingering on her hair before he hitches his linen pants at the knee and claims the chair facing the house. About the glittering ancient lake of our youth behind him, he says nothing, not one word.

How could this man, this *Michael O'Shea*, be my long-lost friend?

"Like a dream, isn't it?" The man pours wine, hoists his own glass aloft: "To the three of us together again!"

The lake is sugared with sails and the occasional froth of a whining motor boat spinning from shore to shore. The water itself appears far cleaner than the murky, dangerous water of our youth. But, then, everything is brighter now, so brilliantly false it hurts my eyes.

I gulp my wine. How long, I wonder, did it take Ellen to mention me in her emails, how long did it take this fellow to start calling me "Laurie" as she does, as Michael O'Shea did all those years ago? Across the table, my sister's fiancé twirls the ring on Ellen's left hand

and fixes his unrelenting alien grin on me. Six months he and Ellen corresponded. Can you call email correspondence? I asked Teresa, but she'd just feigned disgust at my inability to see the romance. Dozens of messages daily, Ellen told me. Texts, DMs, screen after screen of boxed thoughts and desires, the cyber-equivalent of Ula's basement. It was as if they lay inside each other's minds, anticipating, understanding. How natural it all seemed, Ellen told me, plowing past my confusion. And how thrilling, too. No one, she said, again and again, had ever felt so close to her. Should that be a surprise? After all, Michael wasn't a stranger, was he? It's not, she repeated, as if she'd taken up with a stranger. Michael O'Shea was as close as I had ever come to a brother. Wasn't he?

And I had once wished fervently that Michael O'Shea was my brother, mine alone. As always then, I had a plan. I'd worked out all the details and even approached my mother with the idea. *What if*, I asked her, *we traded?* In return for Michael, my parents could send my intrusive sister to the O'Sheas's with their house full of bruising boys. Ellen could move her twin-size canopy bed and her pink-flounced curtains over to the O'Sheas's big brick house. She could take over the room recently vacated by the death of Mr. O'Shea's mother. No longer would we be bothered with Ellen tailing us on her pink bike with the banana seat and the purple streamers. She'd have enough to do at the O'Sheas's, organizing the voluminous bins of Lincoln Logs, helping Mrs. O'Shea cook the mountainous meals those boys demanded.

What I had almost forgotten was how I wanted O'Shea to live with me so badly that I believed we were brothers, separated by error. When Mr. O'Shea was transferred, I wrote long, impassioned letters to Michael about my daily life as if, by keeping him abreast, I could guarantee his return. Haunted by O'Shea, I'd been baldly needy in those letters, berating my friend like a schoolgirl for not writing, until finally Mrs. O'Shea sent me a note on her blue-flowered stationery.

< 108 >

Her kind words, apologizing for Michael's laxity (*He's not much of a writer, honey. And there's baseball season, you know*) shamed me terribly and, appalled, I promptly burned O'Shea's address. O'Shea would not have even needed a room of his own. My lower bunk would have suited him well enough.

———————

Although I am not the slightest bit hungry, I begin to eat again. I cram one delicate sandwich into my mouth even as my hand reaches for another. The sandwich I prefer is the lobster salad on sourdough. The crusts are cut off, the bread is soft and slightly tangy, and the texture, delicate as the Sunday host, is calming. I consume six of the little triangles while this O'Shea explains his latest wedding brainstorm.

"What an interesting idea, Michael. Will it really work?"

"Of course, honey," this stranger reassures Ellen. "People do it all the time. Bundy O'Reilly and Mary Jenkins, the D'Andreases—they all were married on their pools."

I mistake a tuna for a lobster salad. My face twists.

"You don't like the idea, Laurie." My sister notices, of course.

I shrug, my mouth full. The man waits. I swallow hard.

"It sounds perfect, Michael," she says, keeping her eyes on me. With her free hand, she shifts the plate of sandwiches to the far edge of the table just out of my easy reach. I catch the man's eyes just in time to see the briefest narrowing of...what?...irritation?...suspicion?...come and go.

My sister's fiancé picks up a strawberry from the yellow bowl, swivels it between his fingers as if he is about to suggest a complicated betting game that requires only the reddest and most perfect of strawberries. A bee hovers an inch away from his hand, but he pays no attention. Of course, I think, drifting off a little, if he's not real, why would he worry about being stung? The strawberry acts as some

< 109 >

kind of a signal. Ellen, glancing meaningfully at her Internet date, is suddenly on her feet, the platter of sandwiches grasped tightly in her hand. She has decided she must confer with the kitchen staff immediately about the wedding caterer's upcoming visit.

*The kitchen staff.*

"Unbelievable, isn't it?" the man says, his eyes on Ellen's retreating figure, "that we should be here again at the lake?"

"So you remember the boat?"

"Of course, I remember our boat, Laurie. In fact, Ellen and I were just talking about it the other night. As a matter of fact, check this out." He points down the hill toward the lake, where a little blue skiff bobs beside a new dock. He offers me the easy, expectant grin of a man who's studied well for the test.

Should I run him through our teachers and other classmates, through the times we tortured O'Shea's older brothers with practical jokes? Surely something remained separate from Ellen, something that belonged just to the two of us.

The flattening fatigue brought on by my swim and this extended eating session dulls my thinking. I spin my own strawberry in a tabletop puddle of gold wine, and Ula's voice, so familiar these days inside my head, arrives: *Declare yourself, Lawrence,* she says. *You must.*

"Ellen reached you by mistake, didn't she?" I finds myself blurting. "How many Michael O'Sheas must there be? Hundreds, maybe thousands?"

Clouds momentarily closet the sun. The man's features vanish under the shadow of the table umbrella. I am ranting to a faceless figure in a ridiculous suit, a bland pillar of beige linen. Only my host's feet, squirming in their soft, expensive loafers, let me know I'm being heard.

Above us, behind windows so extravagantly tall and wide they seem to reflect the entire blistering world, the outline of my sister is listening intently to an outline of the tidy white-haired woman who scowled at me when we passed through the kitchen. My sister's head is bent to one side. Even from this distance, the beam of Ellen's focused attention is visible. The maid's aloofness cracks into smiles and gestures; she unfurls herself in Ellen's tender light. My sister, I decide, is a conjurer; she births people, brings them into being.

"Okay," I am startled to hear the fellow say, "Okay, I'll play your game a little here, Laurie. Suppose," he says, "that you're right, that I'm not Michael O'Shea, but some online Casanova, a predator who seeks unsuspecting women. What would be my goal? I mean, what the hell would my prize be? I'll be frank with you, Laurie. I happen to love your sister, but she is neither rich nor young nor the possessor of state secrets."

"She's smart," I can't help saying, "and beautiful, and she has a unique and consoling consciousness."

"She is," he agrees, grinning with pleasure. "She does. She always has."

"She is a catch. Any man would be lucky to have her." Something is off with my logic, I realize. I should have this fake O'Shea floating out to sea by now. I try another tack.

"For your books," I mumble. "That's why you'd do it. What if you were running out of ideas? What if your fabulous business was failing miserably? What if you wanted a whole new series? *How to Find a Wife; How to Insinuate Yourself into a New Hometown; Surviving Yourself: How to Forge a New Identity.*" I'm babbling now: *What if? What if? What if?*

The man's balding head turns pink. I am gripping the arms of my chair, ready to rise and defend myself when he lets loose a snorting, bellowing roar that I recognize immediately as belonging to the real

< 111 >

O'Shea's father. Old Man O'Shea, playing pinochle in his basement with his barroom buddies, shaking the living room floor with his convulsive laugh and the uncontrollable coughing fit that inevitably followed. Confused, I avert my face, and my attention is snagged by the blue skiff banging against the dock below.

We'd wrecked our boat, of course, our first time out. Mid-lake, our inexpert repairs began to give way seriously, the tiny sputters of water elbowing through newly opened seams until our ankles were numb with the water that kept rising. We'd come to the lake in the early morning, paddled through mist that dampened our cheeks, our hair dripping down the backs of our necks. No one knew where we were, not even Ellen, although later she would have guessed, would have directed everyone to the empty boatshed, the quiet lake. Barely light and Michael, for once, had taken charge, had barked at me to paddle harder, faster, faster, through the speckled fog toward the lip of black shore where we could just make out a pale pillar of light that I first thought was just the curve of bare beach. As we drew closer, the water almost up to our thighs, our arms still churning like mad, I'd looked up to see the beacon shift right; then left, then right again. Ellen—Ellen with a flashlight! We believed that almost to the minute our oars touched the lake bottom and the mist began to break into thin smoke-like columns around them.

I remember clearly Michael's face, his own subdued astonishment at the empty beach, the vanished light. I remember the speed with which we clambered from the boat, how we fled through the forest and past the shadowy gauntlet of heads. I can picture the two of us, tripping over our own feet, nearly holding hands in our terror at being rescued by a ghost. The almost uncontainable relief of that moment spills over, knocks me off my chair, here on this foreign patio. In another second, I am on my feet, vigorously slapping O'Shea's back as he recovers from his coughing fit.

"Michael?" I begin again, frowning with relief.

"Oh, Laurie," O'Shea grins. "It is you, buddy, isn't it?"

He wipes his eyes, and then before I can catch my breath, he reaches out to clasp my hand. And that's how my sister finally finds us, two old friends, speechless, holding hands with relief, once more by bright water.

< 113 >

# SWALLOW

---

"Spit it out," his mother says, offering her yellow dishtowel as receptacle.

Crumbs dot Bruno's mouth and one cheek as if he's immersed his entire face in his plate, groveling like the seven-year-old animal he is. A born heathen who acknowledges no one's instructions, who is always scavenging, always hungry and never satisfied, Bruno lives the life of a savage, bounding through the neighborhood with sharpened sticks, telling time by the sun, losing articles of clothing every hour so that when he arrives home at dinnertime, famished and cross, he is often bare-chested and sunburned, his bare feet filthy with dry mud. His older brother and sister are supposed to mind him; that goes without saying. But each summer morning, as the aluminum screen door wheezes closed behind them, the brother flies onto his English racer bicycle, the sister beelines it up Church Road to her friend Regina's house, and Bruno is left eyeing the neighbors.

Two doors down, Gilbert is an only child. Across from him, Marcella is one of six sisters, all the rest wan wraiths who prefer a cool sunporch floor to thick puddles of side-yard mud, to the high-grass trail and the creek behind the ball field. Tim and Renau and Skip are a trio of look-alike best friends who haunt the hoop in Tim's driveway. All of them, including Bruno, know how to whistle and sidle up with a plan. All know how to steal through the backyards of the elderly and the childless and the rarely-at-home. As a group, they've discovered a cave beside the creek and have ventured onto the railroad tracks, where they've placed the obligatory pennies and waited for the com-

< 114 >

muter run. They have climbed onto garage roofs, scraping their hands raw on bristled wood edges and asphalt shingles; they have eaten uncooked hot dogs under the rectory hedge while defiling Marcella's crucifix; they have practiced lying like a line of dead bodies in the back of the McCordles's station wagon, playing Hearse; they have sucked dry an entire bramble of honeysuckle vines and chewed a garden of mint leaves to a pulp. They have pilfered handfuls of change from overcoat pockets in front hall closets and taken them to the drugstore freezer case to gorge on Rocket Pops, cramming them down so quickly their eyeballs nearly exploded from the cold rush. (A rare mistake, this turned out to be; Bruno had been punished with a strap in the basement, a lapse of judgment for which he's never forgiven himself.) They have dared each other to eat bugs and drink piss and break high windows in an abandoned glitter factory. They might be the best of friends, but at times they eye each other like strangers, enemies even, and it's then that Bruno sets off on his own.

So it is that early one afternoon in high summer, Bruno is tunneling under a chain-link fence. He has no idea whose fence it is or why it's there, but he hates the sensation of being locked out, and so when he notes the distance between the bottom of the fence and the dusty dirt beneath, he makes a calculation, hunts for and achieves a good flat-edged stick, and manages to widen that distance enough for a wiry small boy to belly beneath.

Bruno would make a very good dog.

He's in scrub grass with no earth beneath it. Instead, his sneakers navigate broken asphalt, which smoothes abruptly into pavement. A ghost road winding through an abandoned lot with pockets of debris, a treasure trove of broken possibilities that seems to go on for a mile before the ground tips downhill and Bruno begins to edge alongside a blind brick building. A series of metallic flashes ahead—sunlit signals—sends him lurching forward, even as his eyes scan the weedy

< 115 >

pavement hoping for everything from arrowheads to a switchblade. Occasionally, he raises his head and sniffs the hot air, which is pleasurably damp and heavy and tinged with the familiar heady scent of urine. He finds a new-ish black comb and a half-full pack of Tiparillos and stuffs both in the deep pockets of his shorts before continuing on, eyes relentlessly scanning. In this manner, head down, he rounds the back corner of the brick building before he's fully aware and so nearly bangs into a green panel van, idling with its back doors open onto a loading dock. The loading dock's ramp is littered with busted crates. Beyond that, framed in the building's open steel doors, two men dressed in dark blue coveralls. Their backs are to Bruno, and they haven't heard him approach, but they are mere feet away, and the air itches with his arrival, the changed scene. One man's head is already lifting, turning.

Bruno is a master of metamorphosis. Around strangers encountered in the wild, he transforms into thin gray smoke, swirling and vanishing before he fully registers, leaving behind only the faintest impression of disturbed air. More than once, he has discerned alien figures slinking along the creek bed or beside the railroad tracks and seeped away well before the others, perfect patsies, gained a clue. To them, it was as if the earth had gulped him down whole. Bruno's problem now is that, beneath the green van's idle, he hears the rumble of another vehicle, this one approaching from behind, from the ruined drive he's just traversed.

Even smoke has limited choices, depending upon the way the wind is blowing, Today, the wind is blowing from two directions at once. A lesser boy would not have even attempted the feat. A lesser boy would choke.

But by the time the car behind him materializes and another man, this one sallow-faced in an old brown suit, emerges, Bruno-as-Smoke is curled in a rubble of plastic and wood stakes, wedged between

< 116 >

rusted oil drums and the ever-present fence. He still has his stick, and if the plastic didn't rustle so, he'd be digging a new exit hole more vigorously, ready once again to become Bruno-as-Dog. He does paw a little at the ground, testing its pliability, poking around for a hollow beneath the chainlink fence. Even in the blasted heat beneath his plastic hideaway, Bruno can feel another shift in the air as the men inside the loading dock grow faces, turning their attention to the space he recently vacated, now fully occupied by the man in the brown suit.

"You sorry bastards," the man greets them in a gravelly voice that interests Bruno. "I bet you think no one knows what you're up to."

The comment confounds Bruno. He is wondering if the man has seen him after all and is warning the others about *him*. He's been squatting, rocking back and forth on his toes, and he briefly loses balance, catching himself by splaying his palms flat on the cindered ground. It's only as he's righting himself that one paw-like hand shifts and brushes against what he took to be another roll of plastic and Bruno realizes he's not alone in his makeshift tent.

---

Oh, where are Bruno's protectors? Shouldn't someone be following the child, supervising, directing? Of course not. A mother might allow a few early morning hours of cereal munching and cartoon watching, only to erupt in a mad sweep that propels the children out of milk-sopped pajamas into shorts and T-shirts and broken-backed Keds and then out the back door with a slam and maybe even a twisted lock behind them. Lunch, yes, they might return for lunch. And before dark. Absolutely. But in-between, work must be done: rugs beaten or vacuumed, floors waxed, bathrooms scrubbed, and cakes baked. Home permanents must be applied, shirts ironed, martinis chilled. The children have the easiest job of all: *amuse yourselves.*

In addition to the older brother (12) and sister (11), Bruno has a far more mysterious and desirable sibling: red-haired, sixteen-year-old Elyse. Early on, she petted baby Bruno, carrying him from place to place at their mother's instruction. When the family began to civilize his infant self, corralling him in a highchair, she fed him by spoon, the only one he allowed to do so. The nest of her strong arms, his fingers tugging on her long red braid, lulled him to sleep even when he vowed at the top of his lungs to everyone else: *No Sleep! No Sleep!* Elyse was, for the first four years of his life, the closest Bruno would get to pure, gut-wrenching love. Naturally, she began to slip away— school, of course, and other lessons: ballet, guitar, French, and now, driving. He had spent ages propped at the screen door, one finger in his mouth, the other methodically ripping a hole in the worn screen, waiting in vain for her timely return. Even now, hardened soul that he is, his sister's appearance can act as a spark on Bruno's heart, widening and enlivening it, so that he is propelled by an unfamiliar desire to follow directions.

While Bruno is squatting beneath a makeshift tent in the high grass of a derelict lot, his Elyse is practicing K-turns with two brothers, both of whom also vie for her affection. Chris is in her grade at school, a baseball player, fair-haired and assured. It's Chris who guides Elyse through the turn and laughs when she spins the wheel and accelerates and the car flips backwards, then frontwards, landing perfectly in place like a police cruiser in a slow-motion movie. Martin, Chris's brother, is a year older, a senior in the fall. It's his car Elyse is swinging from side to side, up and down the quiet avenue that leads to the high school, empty now for the summer holidays except for a few distant figures running on the playing fields. Martin saved for years for this car with its custom midnight blue paint job, and he's claimed the front seat beside Elyse. Screw Chris.

When Martin dreams of Elyse, sometimes they are in this very car, in the backseat, and she is removing every single article of her

< 118 >

clothing so that first he sees her creamy freckled shoulders, then her full soft white breasts. Actually, that's about as far as Martin manages before he explodes. Some days, he can barely even glance at his car's backseat without feeling a cold shudder in his groin.

"Sit back, will ya?" Martin commands his brother, who hangs between him and Elyse like an unwelcome, overly enthusiastic mutt. Most of the time Martin feigns a kind indifference to Elyse, pretending he is along simply to safeguard his vehicle, but every now and then, when Elyse takes a corner far too sharply and Chris makes an exaggerated show of leaning her way, his hands reaching outward to grasp those creamy, near-naked shoulders, Martin gives himself away.

"Cripes, Chris, how the hell is she supposed to drive if you're clinging to her?"

Chris ignores his brother. He is bathed in the athlete's glow, certain of his golden allure. He will win out; he always does. Martin knows his brother thinks him a serious scarecrow, too gangly to catch a girl's eye, too oblique to desire it. He earned the car by being a drudge, working every crappy job that had come his way since he was ten years old. While Chris honed his right arm pitch and practiced a trademark teasing wink in the mirror, Martin cut lawns, swept out the tailor's shop, stacked soda cartons, made bicycle deliveries. In fact, this is the first summer day he's taken off in years and he did it solely for Elyse, whom he met two summers ago when he was trimming her neighbor's bushes and she was minding her beastly younger brother.

For her part, Elyse seems oblivious to the brothers' private battles. She bears a fierce inner cool that Bruno too has inherited. She does not give herself away. Her driving test is in three days; her mother is endlessly preoccupied; her escape plan depends upon this license, and the loan of Martin's car is a boon she will not risk by flirting with Martin's brother. While Chris smirks in Martin's direction, she begins to parallel park, the steering wheel shuddering slightly under her slim

< 119 >

fingers. Martin whispers "mirror," and she easily corrects, allowing a slight downward nod in that anxious boy's direction that thrills him. Her full lips purse and open, purse and open. He nearly groans aloud, imagining the possibilities. If only his brother would go away.

The ferocity of a desperate wish can be electric. Martin's subterranean desire rumbles and roars and becomes a cosmic howl, and even as Elyse slides his quaking car against the curb, the back door is yarded open and Chris is yanked onto the curb by a pair of his baseball teammates.

A grinning snaggletoothed ballplayer sticks his face through Martin's open window and ogles Elyse.

"Pardon us," he smirks. "We'll only be a minute."

On the sidewalk, Chris is huddled in their midst as if he's being congratulated. The wait irritates Elyse even more than it does Martin, so when he leans closely to her and softly issues a command, she does not hesitate.

"*Go*," Martin whispers. "*Drive. Now. Go.*"

The midnight blue sedan peels away from the curb with a shriek that might have been wrung from the tires or from the flabbergasted Chris, who hesitates too long before beginning a comically doomed pursuit by foot while his teammates whoop in derision.

"Jackasses," Martin says. "Feebs."

He has a pocketful of dimes, a slim roll of bills, all meant for his weekly savings deposit, but he decides instead he'll take Elyse to Mission Street to an outdoor café he's passed on his way to work each day. A romantic spot, bohemian in an industrial way. She'll like that. He'll woo her first.

Without Chris playing with her hair, Elyse feels far less constrained. She'd like to snap on the radio and take Martin's car out to the Old Highway and see just how fast it will go. Take a few risks. She rests her left elbow, that long, freckled honey arm, on the open window and steers with one hand, smoothly shifting as she follows Martin's instructions.

"Turn here," he points. "And here."

---

Of course, Bruno hadn't recognized the black plastic covering and stakes as a tent. The lean-to composed of wood scraps and bricks and chunks of broken masonry seemed more trash heap than lodging. And, then again, he'd had only a split second to leap to its shelter. But don't be mistaken; he is not afraid. Bruno has never been afraid. The closest he's come to that emotion was the subdued fury he felt when his father took down the strap in the basement. Now, his eyes strain to see, but it's pitch black beneath the plastic and the air is very close with, he realizes, a faint humming of foreign breathing. He lifts an edge of plastic slowly, soundlessly.

As he does, he hears the man in the suit say, "...and if anyone stops you, you swallow it, you hear. You swallow, you hear. Make the damn stuff disappear."

As if to add emphasis, a car door slams like an exclamation point, and Bruno soon spies the moving edge of a heavy black car.

In the silence that follows, a different voice, lighter, less frantic, drawls: "I ain't swallowing shit."

Another voice pronounces, "No way in hell I'm doing the swallowing. Don't even think that."

Bruno hears the steel door shudder and clang shut. The van's doors are next, and the van itself bellows into life and rumbles from the lot with such speed little pieces of asphalt go flying and ping against the plastic. At precisely the same moment Bruno flees his hideout, but not before yet another voice, a much closer voice, says quite plainly, "If it were me, kid, I'd swallow. You bet I would. But first I'd run like hell."

So Bruno does.

Martin is about to finally make his move, sliding sideways on the bench seat under the pretense of checking the gauges, a random dishonest concern that the oil pressure is rising. His left hand is creeping up behind Elyse's narrow shoulders in her pink-checked haltered dress, and his own breath is mixing with the perfume of her warm skin. For once, Martin is glad he does not have a convertible, that the whole world isn't audience to a yearning so powerful that he is practically levitating, yes, he's navigating air, his skinny butt rising from the seat as he reaches for her, and she is almost, almost within his grasp when, without warning, Elyse brakes hard and Martin rushes forward so that his expectant face hits the dashboard. He tastes blood.

"Oh my god," Elyse breathes, "it's Bruno."

Martin's cheeks are brindled pink. He struggles upright even as Elyse runs the car against the nearest curb. His car, *his* (he realizes) *fragile old* car, shrieks ominously as she slams the transmission into Park. Before he can chastise her, she's run into the street. He follows, of course, what else can he do, although the last thing he ever hoped to do today was kneel beside some beastly half-dead dog cowering on the curb.

But it's not a dog, and it's not half-dead or cowering. Bruno is glowing with triumph. Filthy, reeking from whatever nasty stream ran beneath his hideout, he is celebrating his escape, holding an unlit Tiparillo between his sooty lips and using his new comb to arrange his hair as he imagines the man in the brown suit would, with a high, stylish wave in the front. His bare legs are dusted with soot and yellow dirt; even the scabs look exotic. He couldn't be more pleased with himself, and then, as if to crown the greatness of this adventure, Elyse *drives* up.

# Swallow

―――――――――

Martin cringes when Elyse leads her brother into the sacred backseat. She seems, too, to be promising the creature a ride on the Old Highway straight to the riverbank. Martin can think of plenty of possibilities along the riverbank, but none include this seeping, cigar-chomping delinquent. At last, he puts his foot down.

"No," he tells Elyse as she pauses outside the driver's door. "We're taking the kid home."

A hard edge creeps into his voice, but it's only when her eyes widen and narrow that he realizes he's holding her hand. Tightly.

"But I promised," she begins half-heartedly.

"I'll take care of it," Martin says, releasing her hand slowly, allowing the edge of his thumb to stroke her palm as he does. It's a magic move. Elyse sees him emerge from the trembling fog that's surrounded him, and he looks nothing like the cloistered wretch she might have imagined, another begging boy doomed to ridicule. Martin has folded up that self and kicked it into the corner. Elyse is impressed.

"We'll take a drive, okay?" he says. "You and me."

And the empty back seat, he thinks.

"Sure," she says, and the agreement charges them both.

The car keys have migrated to his left hand, and so, with a tiny twitching smile of her own, Elyse slides across the driver's seat almost into Martin's former position.

Martin reaches into his pocket, then opens the back door. He leans closely to Bruno, stifling his own gag reflex. Elyse doesn't even turn her head as Martin slides a river of coins, a tiny silver waterfall, into Bruno's lap, all the while holding young Bruno's gaze.

"No highway, today, kid," he says.

The "kid" settles Bruno immediately, and he secures this new

< 123 >

unforeseen booty in his pocket. He doesn't complain at all when Martin drives him to the end of his block and simply waits until Bruno scrambles out.

"Hey, Bruno," Elyse calls him back. Her hand floats out through the window, and without any real reluctance, he deposits the slim Tiparillo box in her clean white palm.

---

"Wash your hands," his mother yells. And though he lathers hard and actually discolors the sink as he rinses, his mother eyeballs him as he approaches the kitchen. He ignores her to confront a grilled cheese sandwich that he reckons, two-fisted, might be consumed in one enormous bite. He makes the effort, and the back of his throat expands. His eyes tear. He writhes in his seat. Bruno-as-Snake. The sandwich consumed, he allows a throat-searing, triumphant belch and a bounce upon his seat. His sister, the non-Elyse, gags with disgust.

And his brother, ever traitorous, must interfere: "Bruno's jingling," he says. "He's been in the coat closet again, Mom."

Bruno's protestations could not be more genuine. His jaw drops in real hurt. Yet when the teakettle screams and his mother's attention is briefly diverted, Bruno's hand shoots into his pocket, and the evidence of Martin's bribe flows into his mouth to the astonishment of his siblings, who have ignored him once too often and whose hysteria strikes Bruno as downright comical.

"Spit it out," his mother says, offering her yellow dishtowel as receptacle.

But it's too late. Bruno has learned the lesson for today. He swallowed.

# MADAME IDA

Although Cloris and Hattie Finnerty, Ida's young neighbors, can be depended upon to feed Ida's cat and bring in the newspaper, they also like to riffle through her mail when she is away, culling out the magazines and catalogs they fancy and leaving the rest in a tidy throwaway stack in the milk bin inside the kitchen door. Bills and the rare letter are carelessly mixed within the pile, and are, as Ida has discovered from past experience, exceptionally easy to overlook. So, on returning from a visit to her sister Joanie, Ida combs patiently through the little girls' rejects, and in this way she finds, slipped between the pages of a glossy four-page advertisement for a foreign language program, a flat, pale blue envelope with a sketched flower border addressed to her only child, Dave. The printed black letters are loopy and aggressive, a little alphabetical brass band, cymbals and horns blasting out her son's name as if to accentuate a second message, a bright red sticker plastered crookedly along the bottom of the envelope:

*Urgent. Immediate attention, please!*

Over a year ago, Dave had given up on his six-year struggle for a PhD in physical science and shocked everyone by finagling a position at an all boys' school in France. There he began teaching English and, in record time, also married the school secretary, a divorcée named Marie-Therese. The wedding party was too hastily assembled, apparently, to allow for Ida's attendance. The couple sent her an attractive announcement—ecru edged in gold—which was Dave's way of saying, once and for all, that he wasn't coming home.

Her son does not like Ida to forward his mail. He would like her to destroy the occasional piece with his name on it, ripping each envelope into tiny squares and scattering the pieces into the trash. But those other letters don't smell faintly of lilac bath powder, nor do they bear the slight imprint of a teacup as this one does. On the back of those envelopes, no one has doodled a caricature of Dave himself, complete with his new tiny eyeglasses, the ones that make him look like an intelligent insect. The drawing portrays the cartoon Dave caught in a forest of slim birch-like trees, each bearing a semblance of his own face. One of the cartoon Dave's hands is outstretched toward the envelope's flower border. A delicate ink trumpet vine curves sensuously toward his open palm, barely missing contact. Ida is startled by how closely the drawing resembles her view of her son. It's as if someone has rendered the heart of Dave as she sees it.

The mystery deepens: the envelope lacks a return address, and even the stamp has been removed, leaving only the faint smudge of an unintelligible postmark. A careful slice with the letter opener reveals that it is, indeed, an empty envelope. No, this isn't an ordinary solicitation, she decides, but an entire personality occupying her kitchen counter, caterwauling for attention. Her suitcase still squats on the back porch, and she hasn't yet removed the blue blazer she wears for traveling, but Ida remains in reverie, the envelope still in hand, until a loud internal mewling stirs her and she puts the envelope aside to consider the subject of supper.

Last night, Joanie had taken her to an East Indian restaurant that recently opened on the edge of her Indiana suburb. They'd driven twelve miles to the restaurant, which was situated in an old semi-abandoned mall next to a grocery store called Sub-Rite. Her sister dragged her into Sub-Rite, as well, to buy a carton of cigarettes. Apparently one of the charms of the East Indian restaurant was that they allowed smoking "everywhere." Or so Joanie claimed, although Ida knew that couldn't be true. There were laws now about smoking sections. She, herself, would kick the habit if she could, and she often asked to sit in non-smoking sections to force herself to be good.

Something was wrong with the supermarket's lighting. The fluorescent bulbs not only flickered, they flashed from time to time as if an itinerant photographer was at work recording the shabbiness of the place. The carton of cigarettes Ida's sister bought was crushed at one end. All the cartons were crushed, but each cost only two dollars and sixty-nine cents.

"That can't be right," Ida whispered to Joanie as the checker, bare-chested under his overalls, made slow change from a five, his lips moving silently as he counted every penny.

"It's a discount store," her sister stage-whispered back, "a bargain palace."

Ida looked around then—as best she could with the lights popping in her eyes. Except for those lights, of course, and the dirt floor where the linoleum had broken away, the Sub-Rite could have passed as a normal supermarket—at first. But Ida soon noticed that the oversized cans that lined the shelves were deeply dented and the packages, all with the same relentless gray wrapping, half-smashed. It was disturbing how the store, which seemed so familiar in its contours, transformed itself before her eyes into something altogether different and alien.

While Ida was squinting at the shelves, a line of women materialized at the end of aisle in front of her and began to weave their way toward the front of the store. One extremely large woman was in the lead. Dressed in a paisley muumuu, swirls of tangerine and fuchsia and robin's egg blue, she commandeered a twelve-wheeler flatbed cart that spanned the width of the aisle. Behind her, two more large women led a procession of children, all girls, all in long brilliant bedspreads of skirts, their hair looped in heavy buns beside their ears.

"It's a Princess Leia convention," she whispered, nudging her sister.

"Farfans," Joanie pronounced, staring with her.

Ida knew they were being incredibly rude, but she, for one, couldn't tear her eyes away. The children kept coming and coming like the dandelions in the scrub grass that surrounded the mall. There must have been a dozen girls of varying ages moving up the aisle behind the older women, matching their stately, very unchildlike pace.

"*Farfans?*" she whispered, riveted by the lead woman who, Ida could see now, had a ring of blue flowers woven into her elaborate hairdo. Without pausing, the woman offered Ida a gentle, almost amused gaze as the procession passed. Mesmerized, Ida took a few steps forward and nearly tripped over a curling corner of linoleum. She would have, too, if that same woman hadn't left her place to gracefully catch Ida's arm and set her straight. Ida felt almost as if she'd been tucked back into her spot beside Joanie, who Ida noticed with surprise was smirking at her.

"Patchouli oil," Joanie sniffed as the procession moved away from them. "Haven't smelled that in years."

"What are Farfans?" Ida asked.

"It's a new religion," the checker weighed in, diverting Ida's attention momentarily with the proximity of his bare, pimpled shoulder.

"Yeah, right," her sister said. "Bud Farfan's religion. He used to be the county sheriff, Ida, a land developer on the side, a local shark. But he got too big for his britches, made a few too many pronouncements about his irreplaceable status, and he was trounced in the election a few years back. The defeat drove him nuts; he purely couldn't believe he hadn't been chosen. After the third recount, they barred him from the courthouse, and he disappeared. Two months later, he appeared back in the news, standing on a downtown street corner with a sheaf of songs he'd composed on his autoharp and a little harem of women, all swearing Farfan was the Messiah, that he'd been cast out by his

< 128 >

enemies as predicted. Of course, no one seemed to care a whit. The authorities ignored him and after a while, he wrote a letter to the *Gazette*, saying he was retiring. That old Nixon trick: *You won't have Bud Farfan to kick around anymore.* Only Farfan's letter was far more gracious. Really, Ida, you'd think he was somebody. And all these women *flocked* to him."

"Like the disciples," the clerk put in.

"Or gold diggers," Joanie said with a trace of irritation. "You know that new condo complex out by the lake, Ida? The one you noticed from the plane? Farfan, the developer, built that, and now they all live there. And that," she added, nodding toward the head woman in the procession, the woman who'd righted Ida, "is his Queen."

"God has a queen?"

The clerk, who'd been leaning uncomfortably close to Ida and Joanie, muttered conspiratorially, "Farfan *thinks he does,* from what I've heard. But he's retired now," he said, pointedly to Joanie, flaunting his superior knowledge. "He's not even living out there anymore, they say. Cashed in his pension, signed the condos over to her, and left the state, they say. No one has seen him in months, not a word from him, either. The *Queen,* though, she's not going anywhere just yet, not with that bunch."

Ida couldn't wrap her mind around the story. "God's retired?" she asked.

"Missing, more like it," the checker said. He leaned in closely: "Something's not right there."

Ida began to sputter a question, but Joanie sighed, "Give it up, honey. None of it makes any sense. I just wish they'd leave the children out of it."

From this distance, however, the girls appeared remarkably content as they followed the line of women, imitating the movement of their fingertips brushing the worn gray wrappers as if the material were silken. That the sensuality of the women seemed at odds with the idea of a cult religion only amazed Ida further. She turned for one last look just as a long florescent tube exploded by the produce aisle. The store plunged into a deeper level of dinginess. The last Ida saw of the Farfan women was a group of shadows sashaying into the gloom, their hands reaching slowly and serenely for bruised cantaloupes and cellophane bags of sprouted potatoes.

———————

At the East Indian restaurant next door, dapper men in pink and cream-colored silk shirts served Ida and Joanie plate after plate of beautiful food—golden pakoras, tandoori chicken stained that peculiar red, crisp samosas—until not one spare inch remained on the stiff white tablecloth. The lights were low, the room hazy and smoke-filled; taped sitar music twanged softly. Ida and Joanie pulled out their half-crushed cigarettes, and the handsome little men rushed toward them with huge glass ashtrays and thick books of matches. The sisters drank two Manhattans apiece and ate heartily. When Ida told a joke she'd been harboring for weeks, Joanie went into spasms of loud laughter that rocked the overfilled table and sent the waiters scurrying towards them, which made the sisters laugh even harder.

Oh, they had fun together.

But later that night a terrific pain in Ida's stomach forced her awake.

She had been dreaming that she was giving birth to Dave again. He pitched and rolled inside her, unwilling to follow the usual plan, and she woke up with the startling sensation of a fist emerging from her throat. She and Joanie collided in the hallway. Joanie took one look at Ida and veered down the stairs toward the powder room while Ida barely made it to the upstairs bathroom. Afterwards, they both lay on the nubby blue carpet of Joanie's living room, covered with the green and yellow crocheted blankets Joanie had inherited from their mother. Ida had managed to grab a couple of mixing bowls and a roll of paper towels, and they spent the wee hours of her departure day alternately dozing and retching together in a terrible duet.

---

On her drive home from the airport Ida confirmed that at least half the Sub-Rite cigarettes in each pack were broken. Not a bad thing in her opinion. She's smoked several half-cigarettes since her flight landed, and she feels a little smug about them, as if she has finally managed to cheat her habit a little. They taste a little peculiar, like a foreign candy, but Ida is rapidly growing used to their sweet, musty taste. In fact, already she likes it much more than that of her more acrid regular brand.

In her midnight kitchen, she lights yet another stub and considers again the sketch of Dave. Ida can almost sense his exasperation but, as always, her son leaves her at a loss. She cannot guess at even his cartoon's motives. Is his hand straining to cherish the swelling curve of the flower or to crush it? Cigarette smoke lazes around the bedside lamp and she can hear Dave's pretend hacking, his struggles to open a window. She can almost *see* Dave, his pinched face, a concrete chastisement of her bad habits.

*What is it,* she thinks, *that effects that reversal, that puzzling inversion of parent and child?* David, her son—the ferocious toddler with a fire engine fixation, the clumsy, beefy boy, the stunned and tender adolescent—had waded into the know-it-all, fractious shallows of early adulthood, expecting to walk on water. Instead, he was pulled down by the undertow. At nearly thirty, he is still mired in cynicisms. He sucks them relentlessly, an endless mouthful of little green sour balls. She had been too respectful of his budding opinions, she realizes in retrospect. She'd given them a teasing credence, deferred more than she should have in an effort to offset her

< 131 >

late husband Jack's snorting disbelief. Jack, who liked to argue, to mix it up a little. She couldn't get it through her head that those other versions of Dave were gone forever, not just temporarily subsumed by the humorless man who had replaced them. She had favored only an occasional joshing and found too late that her merry acquiescence allowed David to closet himself seemingly indefinitely with the paltry, baneful spirit of righteousness.

The envelope flutters to her lap, and Ida snaps awake, reads once more her son's name.

*Hey*, the envelope screams. *Urgent, remember?*

What do you do with a message like that, especially when your son is gone, clear on the other side of the world, married to a foreigner with a foreign stepchild who calls you not Gran or Grandmama, or even Grand-Mere, but Madame Ida?

When Ida telephones, almost always on a weekend, she can often hear the sound of a television blaring a sports game, so the first Christmas, she sent the stepson Michel a basketball, remembering how much Dave had lived for the hoop and net over the garage.

*Thank you, Madame Ida*, the child had written dutifully (in English, no less), *for the big, brown basketball, which bounces excellently on the road.*

*Mrs. Ida*, she grumbled to herself, making the loosest of translations. Made her sound like a lonely neighbor woman, the kind of queer foreign soul who invites children inside for rock-hard coconut cookies and milk gone off.

"Of course he knows it's a basketball. They just don't play it as much here, Mother," Dave sighed over the phone, explaining how young Michel—something of a practical joker himself, Ida discerned—had gone on to sprain the big toe on his poor pigeon-toed left foot while using the basketball to practice his soccer game. Marie-Terese, Dave insinuated, had not been pleased and neither, in truth, had he.

*Coconut cookies, again,* Ida thought, clutching the phone to her ear.

And she can't get the hang of the time difference, either. She doesn't think it's such a big deal to wake him from time to time. Her son's days continually rush ahead of hers. A call in the middle of the night seems to average out the distance between them somehow. She's tried to explain this to Dave, turning it into a joke, his addled mother, but he doesn't get it.

"Mother, you once taught math. You worked in a bank, for Christ's sake. We're talking simple arithmetic here!"

She hears in his voice the terror of her eventual disintegration, his looming responsibility: *Don't make me come back,* he seems to cry.

Yet when Ida wakes from a fitful sleep that night, and the clock says two in the morning, she instinctively knows her timing is right for once. The inversion is too neat; if she should be asleep, Dave surely must be awake. Michel answers the phone and understands not one word of the French she so carefully pronounces from her little phrase book.

"Pardon," he says, again and again, "oui, pardon."

Finally she gives up: "It's Madame Ida, honey," she tells him.

With that, the boy begins chattering in his own remarkable English. Amazingly, Ida understands him, although his words seem to arrive in stages, a fast unintelligible first impression, followed gradually by meaning that gives final discernible shape to the words. It's like listening in slow motion, layers building upon hazy layers.

"Hubert is at school, too bad," Michel says, and Ida understands that both Dave, who has taken to using his middle name, Herbert—*Hugh-bear* to Michel—and Marie-Therese are at a faculty meeting. Michel's voice is plumbed with regret and relief. Regret, Ida supposes, that she has finally gotten it right and called during the day's prime hours, and relief that Dave (Hubert) is not at home. She can't imagine what it must be like to have her son as a parent. Would he keep his stepson pinned in a chair while he pontificated against computer games or public welfare systems or, perhaps, the many shortcomings of his own upbringing? She hears Michel's barely restrained sigh of pleasure and recognizes it from the days when she and Jack would come home and find that teenage Dave had plans for the evening and had in fact already gone out.

*You can love someone with all your heart,* Ida thinks, *and still be damn glad when you don't have to listen to him.*

"It's about a letter that's come," she tells Michel.

Now the child is silent. She wonders if he thinks she's talking about his thank you note.

"Hello? Michel, are you still there? I don't mean the one you sent. This letter came for Dave, and I was hoping to talk to him, that maybe he might like this letter sent along. It's really pretty wonderful." She feels an inexplicable weight of tears enter her voice, giving it an old lady's quaver.

Michel is grieved, but he must go. He apologizes profusely.

"I will leave your message for Hubert," the boy promises, and then adds—touchingly, Ida thinks—"I am sorry for you." His tone is so softly solicitous that as she replaces the phone in its cradle, an unaccustomed frisson of pleasure runs down her spine.

———

In the morning, Ida finds herself sleeping on the edge of the bed as if her dreams have pushed her there. Not her dreams, she soon realizes, but her old cat sprawled out beside her. He is a true cat, easily seduced into believing in his own grandeur, and Ida imagines the Finnerty girls have been tucking him in between her sheets. Now, she is the interloper in her own bed. He smells awfully sweet, too, as if the girls have been dosing him with scented toilet water from her bathroom cabinet while she was away. She would have thought the cat would abhor such attentions, but he's thrilled to pieces by them. When whispering begins on the patio outside Ida's window, he springs over Ida and scrambles to the kitchen to wait for the girls who overfill his breakfast bowl.

The Finnerty girls have a perfectly acceptable backyard with a jungle gym and a knotted rope swing and a long hilly swath of dandelioned lawn ideal for rolling down. Nonetheless, Cloris, their leader, has declared a preference for Ida's back garden. She swoons over the rose arbor and the tiny murky pond Ida dug herself. The pond has one anemic lily pad and a multigenerational family of frogs, who inspire lengthy fairy tales written by Cloris, wherein the Finnertys (specifically, the youngest, Jemma) frequently stand in for princesses withholding necessary kisses while frogs are pressed against their prim pink mouths.

Today, the Finnertys are playing Mass. On Ida's patio table, an open bag of Hearthside's Seed and Grain bread, the Finnertys' least favorite. Cloris, using an Atlantic City souvenir shot glass from Jack's basement bar, is stamping out hosts. She grinds out each circle of bread, then passes it to Hattie, who flattens it in her palm with her fist. Once they amass a good-sized pile, the girls stack the hosts in a martini glass. The two remaining Finnerty girls kneel on the patio steps. While Cloris moves from Jemma to Ellie, slipping flattened disks of bread on their tongues, Hattie follows with a second martini glass, this one brimming dangerously with grape juice that slops down the little girls' chins. Briefly, Ida feels the weight of sacrilege, but she remembers too how she and Joanie and their brother Eddie had done the same as kids, only they'd used Wonder Bread, followed by flat ginger ale in a gold-rimmed cordial glass.

Watching the girls sip from Jack's martini glass drives Ida to the kitchen. For the first time since her arrival home, she notices a slew of new drawings on the refrigerator door. Cloris's sketches—moon-faced girls with almond eyes and pursed red mouths, girls dressed in flared skirts with little snap pocketbooks in their paw-like hands—surround Ida's single photograph of Dave with his new family: Michel, the bespectacled, long-haired stepson and Marie-Terese, a heavy blonde with short fringed hair and a seriously snotty expression around her pronounced overbite. Ida's still considering the photograph when a voice at her elbow says, "You should get a dog."

"I have a cat," Ida says, motioning toward the brazen creature nuzzled in Cloris's skinny arms. "And I did have a dog once."

Actually, the dog had belonged to her son. A dear old corgi, he had managed to mellow even Dave. Ida has photos of the whole grateful family wrapped around that dog in an album somewhere. She'd place a bet that Cloris has already ferreted out that album and perused it to her heart's content, no doubt floored by the vision of Ida surrounded by a family who appeared to be gloriously content.

"Then a job," Cloris continues. "You should get a job."

"I had one, honey. I'm retired now, you know that."

"I'd bet you'd be good at lots of things," the girl goes on as if she hasn't heard. "You cook good and grow a lot of flowers."

Now all the girls are in the kitchen, staring past the orange juice carton in Ida's hand to the unopened liter of Pepsi on the refrigerator's top shelf.

"You can drive," Hattie points out.

"And be a mommy," Jemma chirps. "Right, Cloree, you said she was a mommy, too? Right?"

"Oh, please," her sister Ellie says, rolling her eyes.

"My little boy is all grown up," Ida says, but the girls don't seem to be listening.

"Hattie, honey," Ida reaches for the liter of Pepsi, "Why don't you grab some more glasses from the cabinet there?" Hattie is the capable Finnerty: nurse to Cloris's doctor, secretary to her boss.

"Or a grandmommy," Jemma interrupts with excitement. "You're not a grandmommy, are you?" She leans her whole body against Ida's knee and tips her head back to meet Ida's gaze.

Jemma has the sweet-smelling plumpness and sleepy confidence of a youngest child. Ida feels an urge to gather this little one into her lap. She takes down the photograph of Dave and his new family and holds it in her hand. She considers telling them about Michel, but they've probably already scrutinized his image anyway, rejecting him as any kin of Ida's.

"Oh, please," Ellie says, clutching her flyaway brown hair with two hands as if she will have to pull it out right there if her sister does not stop talking. Ida can imagine dramatic Ellie in five years, her eyes ringed black with eyeliner, a Chinese character tattooed in black ink on her shoulder.

"Maybe you should call him," Cloris tells Ida, looking at the photograph. And all the little girls, sipping their Pepsi with ice cubes, nod in encouragement.

---

"Halloo, Halloo." Dave's voice sounds extraordinarily nasal, but not half-asleep as it usually does. He sighs heavily when he hears his mother's voice.

"It's one-thirty in the morning here, Mother," he says.

"And you're up!" She is so intent on pulling the letter for Dave out of her nightstand drawer that she misses some of what he says:

"...Michel left a note."

"Yes, he said he would."

"He said he'd leave a note? Mother, what are you talking about?"

"Well, this letter, of course." She begins waving the envelope in her hand as if it would make her visible to him, but Dave has no interest, even after she's explained.

"Wait until you see it," she says. "It'll kill you, the likeness."

"Do you know what you forwarded to me last time, Mother?" he says, not waiting for her reply. "Let me inform you: Two pleas for money from questionable charities, each including a gluey pile of address stickers printed with my name and *your* address. A circular advertising a sale of repossessed cars in New Jersey. I was also invited to become a charter subscriber to a new magazine for dog lovers, and to join a Label-of-the-Month Club (the "enclosed" samples were missing, of course). And St. Bridget's would like to encourage me to increase my weekly tithing, which as you may know, Mother, would be impossible since I've never actually been a parishioner."

"David, perhaps I haven't described this well," she persists. "The letter is marked 'Urgent.' It's artistic, too. It looks...well, it looks intimate."

"Dave," she adds, "it smells like flowers."

Her voice sounds a trifle overwrought to her, but, as if to urge her on, the letter trembles a little in her hand.

"Mother," he says, his voice choppy with frustration, "listen to me and listen carefully, I do not want this letter or any other. I'm sure it's a marketing ploy of some kind. Open it, throw it out, I don't care." He pauses, and Ida feels sure he is about to tell her something else, something more about the letter, about himself.

"Look, Marie-Therese is frantic, Mother. I must get off the phone, she's waiting for Michel to call," he says, wearily.

"This late?" Ida says. "I thought you said it was the middle of the night there."

"I told you, Mother. Michel's run away. At first, we thought it was another of his jokes, but his room's cleaned out. He's gone."

"But I just spoke to him," Ida exclaimed. "He didn't say a word about it."

"I'm not mentioning that to Marie-Therese, Mother." Dave's voice dropped to a whisper. "She's annoyed with me enough as it is. I can't imagine what she'd say if she found out Michel talked with you just before he left her."

"David, that makes no sense."

"Listen, Mother, I'd appreciate it if you wouldn't call for awhile," his voice thinned even further so that Ida could barely hear him. "Michel's probably at his father's house, and if he really will be away for some time...well, it might not be a bad thing. We need this time to ourselves. It won't help anything at all if you keep calling this way."

"Now, Dave," Ida begins, about to protest this view of her constant harassment.

But he cuts her off: "I must be firm here, Mother," he says, and just like that, they are disconnected.

———

Ida doesn't throw out Dave's envelope. Instead, she tucks it, muffled under a magazine on the hall table where, the following day, it is joined by a second one, also with its stamp removed. Here the illustrated Dave is far less ambiguous. Surrounded by test tubes and a frothing black saucepan, he has been transformed into a mad scientist. His curly brown hair, always a trial to him, flies out in all directions. His eyes, behind blue tinted safety glasses, glare red, and his mouth is set in a grim clench that bares a set of pointed teeth. Rings of smoke rise from the bubbling potion and hover behind Dave's head, giving the impression that he, too, is steaming. The image is both alarming and, Ida concedes, extremely funny. Once again, the letter bears David's name and a label. The new sticker reads:

*Contents under pressure. Open at once.*

Well, she has to laugh. This is Dave all right. Simmering. A cork about to pop. She leaves the second letter beside the first and telephones Joanie, distracted only slightly by the arrival of the Finnerty girls, home from school and now intent on a new project in Ida's backyard.

"Ida!" Joanie says. "I was about to call you! Guess what? They found his truck. That dope in the Sub-Rite was right."

"Whose truck?"

"Bud Farfan's. All this time, the women said he'd taken his Ford and driven away to the Southwest. But he left without a word to his ex-wife or kids, and his maintenance checks stopped coming. His brother-in-law went poking about and found the truck, parked off the access road by the lake. The Queen says she doesn't know a thing about it. 'Look,' she said, waving the signed papers Farfan left, handing the condos over to her. 'As long as we are here,' she told the police, "*he* is here.' Now, what could that mean?"

While Joanie details the story of Farfan's disappearance, Ida lights a sweet Sub-Rite stub and observes the garden scene from her bedroom window. The Finnerty girls have found themselves a lost dog. Beside the frog pond, Cloris stuffs the poor animal's hind legs into a pair of frilly white underpants, while Hattie, Ellie, and Jemma hover by their sister, awaiting their turns with a little white nightgown that Ida suspects belongs to Jemma. As she watches, they clothe the terrier and then tip him upside down into the frog pond. His overlarge head disappears into the murk, his little legs whirl in the air.

Ida lays the phone over her shoulder and hurriedly opens her window.

"Girls?" she calls out. "Is that dog okay?"

"He has a pagan soul," Jemma shouts to Ida, her dimpled face fraught with concern.

"And a past life," adds Ellie. He'd been called Lil' Bit, but Chuck, she tells Ida, is the name the Finnerty girls are christening the dog.

Already, Hattie is wrapping the dog in a towel and Cloris has disappeared, no doubt to find a dry outfit.

"...but his family," Joanie is saying, "they don't trust the Queen at all, you see. They're insisting the police investigate further."

"Suicide, they think?"

"Or murder. And the Queen and her gals are getting death threats."

"Death threats!"

Ida distinctly hears a series of tiny clicks on the line.

"Cloris, honey, if that's you on the line, you need to hang up now."

The phone clicks again in response.

"Well, mysterious notes," Joanie continues.

"They're not the only ones." Ida tells her about Dave's letters, then about Michel's running away and, haltingly, Dave's injunctions against her calls. She doesn't mention that since then, she's been too low to do much more than watch the Finnerty Show from her window, but her sister's no fool.

———————

Beginning the next day, Joanie telephones Ida each afternoon and, to the frequent accompaniment of Cloris's eavesdropping clicks, delivers new pieces of the Farfan mystery: how, for instance, the lake has been dredged, yielding only the usual tires and an old bicycle, nothing linked to the ex-Messiah; how a safety deposit box in his name was discovered in a tiny branch office of the bank, but contained only a few old photos and Farfan's completely average final report card from the police academy. Then, finally, this news: the footlocker under a horse blanket, crammed into a crawl space in the Queen's own condo.

"Well, they think she offed him. Either that or he fled buck naked. They found his clothes. Folded and stacked, neat as a pin. His old sheriff's badge on top. Even his shoes, Ida. Those shiny black wing tips he was so proud of. Oh, and the Queen, she's not concerned at all," Joanie says. " 'He was no longer that person,' she says. 'It makes sense he'd discard those trappings.' She's in deep, though, Ida. They have Social Services out there, interviewing the children."

"Well, that's just terrible," Ida says, "using the children like that." Her voice shakes with disapproval. She has, she realizes now, come to appreciate Farfan's Queen, alone now with her girls, released from weight of Farfan's mission. That appreciation must have been roiling inside her, because hours later Ida awakes, dry-mouthed and heart-sore, from a nap on the couch, she's overcome with a sudden desire to make another telephone call. She has to make four separate calls to Directory Assistance, trying every variation of possible names she can think of before the right number emerges, and though it's late, near ten o'clock in Indiana, she can't stop herself. And even though no real person picks up, a message plays and it feels as if it's just for her. Dulcet tones of regret mixed with blessings. Twice more that night she punches in the numbers to hear the peculiar brand of solace that comes from a wronged mother whose generosity knows no bounds.

"I hope she did give him the push," she tells Joanie the next afternoon, a strange fierceness in her voice. "Clearly, he never deserved her."

"Ida," her sister says after a short pause, "honey, you haven't been drinking, have you?"

"You tell me if you think I'm wrong," Ida says. "I'm not, am I? It can't have been easy. Living with a messiah, I mean."

There's another pause while Joanie considers. Ida continues.

"The constant adoration. He must have demanded that, don't you think?"

"Oh, I'd bet he needed to be continually shored up," Joanie says.

"All that community skepticism. There are always doubters, you know. That's got to bring a messiah down. And the sense of impending doom—'*The End of the World is Upon Us!*' Lord knows that must have taken a toll."

"He had to be right all the time."

"I'm sure he never listened."

"No sense of humor, no wiggle room for mistakes."

"A bit of a stiff," Joanie agrees.

"A couple of small mistakes and all those years of devotion..."

"She's better off without him," Joanie concludes gently.

"Do you think?" Ida asks. Inexplicably, her cheeks are damp with tears. She must have been rubbing her eyes with Dave's mail still clutched in her hand. The paper is wet; the lettering starting to smear.

"Oh, honey," her sister croons, causing Ida to smile through her tears. "One thing I am sure of, the real messiah will always love his mother."

---

One week goes by, another. Rain, mud, sun. Regardless of the weather, the Finnertys' visits remain constant, as if they are keeping vigil over her. More than once, Ida looks up from a magazine or a bit of sewing to glimpse a Finnerty or two staring at her—through a window, even from her own hallway.

"You kids need to knock," she's told them. "It's just manners, you know."

But they don't; they just appear. A moving cadre of visible guardian angels. One afternoon, as she's mulling over one of Dave's summer camp projects, the inevitable clay ashtray, she sees Cloris slipping out of her bedroom, down the hall, and out the dining room's sliding glass door. *Really*, she thinks to herself, *these girls are going too far*. She tries to call Meg Finnerty, her neighbor, their mother. Meg answers the phone, but just as she does, Ida gets a hitch in her throat and, for a long moment, can't speak.

"I've had enough of these calls," Meg howls into the silence. "Do you think I have time to wait for you to harass me?" The phone is slammed into the receiver so violently that a little pop resounds in Ida's eardrum. The upside is that her throat clears. The downside: the Finnerty girls remain on guard.

The next afternoon, she tries again, and this time manages to holler out Meg's name before the torrent begins.

"Meg! Meg!" she shouts into the phone, "It's Ida from next door."

A long pause ensues, and just as Ida is wondering whether Meg's put the phone down on her, she hears a series of tiny wheezes and realizes Meg Finnerty is crying.

"Hey," Ida tries, gently. "Meg, I didn't mean to upset..."

"I *can't*," Meg gulps out. "I *can't do this anymore*. And you! *You* should know better than to call me."

And, once again, she disconnects herself from Ida abruptly.

The Finnerty girls are hanging from Ida's trees. They are fairies, and Chuck is some kind of a troll who causes all of them, especially Jemma, to squeal with feigned terror when he meanders under their tree. Cloris, on the branch above Jemma, stands and bounces so that Jemma's more slender bough shakes perilously. It's not a bad time to interrupt.

"Girls!" Ida calls out, "come on in here."

They'll stay for supper, she decides. She makes them cheesesteaks and oven fries and pours great big glasses of Pepsi-Cola over crushed ice. Afterwards, they make chocolate sundaes and eat them cross-legged in front of Ida's old console television. Chuck takes the rug, hardly noticing the foul looks Ida's cat sends him. At some point, Jemma climbs onto Ida's lap and, eyes half-closed, sucks her thumb.

The whole evening, Cloris holds back, but finally, when it's clear they're all fading, she gathers her sisters.

"We have homework," she tells Ida, as if they need an excuse to go home.

Ida is bathed and in bed, every light in the house off save for her bedside lamp, when her phone rings.

"I could charge you with kidnapping," Meg Finnerty whispers into Ida's ear.

"You think?" Ida says. "Maybe they kidnapped me? They outnumber me, you know."

"There are a lot of them," Meg agrees. "You should see their clothes. They fling them all over the place. It's knee-deep over here. I've been folding wash since two this afternoon."

"I'll bet you have, honey."

"And the food. I have all those lunches yet to make for tomorrow."

Ida clucked a little in sympathy.

"Their father's useless. He's on another so-called business trip, you know."

"I did not," Ida says.

"Cloris didn't..."

"She did not."

"She knows everything, that girl."

"So I suspect," Ida sighs.

"I'm really not a crazy person."

"Of course not."

"God, they *love* cheesesteaks. How did you know?"

"You'll be fine," Ida tells Meg. "I promise you that."

"You, too," Megs says softly, to Ida's great surprise. "They love you, you know."

———————————

The following afternoon, a Friday, three o'clock comes and goes, and Ida's backyard remains deserted. She guesses that Meg has finally gathered up her energy and her girls and taken them off for a round of dentist appointments or shoe shopping. Ida reclaims her garden and becomes engrossed in the tedious task of pulling out the crabgrass growing between her irises. Now and then she comes across a noxious pile, evidence of Chuck the dog, who is this moment sleeping on the sunny corner of her patio in a pink-striped undershirt that Ida saw on Jemma not that long ago. It's nearly time for Joanie's daily call, but Ida has no news for her. No more uncommon letters have arrived for Dave. She's kept her itchy fingers off the telephone keypad. She is hardly even aware of her own tears, until she realizes that the far-off huffing she hears is actually coming from her. When she comes to, blowing her nose in a tissue and castigating herself for her own silliness, even the dog has vanished, leaving her completely alone.

The quiet pierces Ida, who decides abruptly to go for a walk. The trees are starting to look filled in again, browning clusters of lacy flowers giving way to glossy leaves. An early afternoon rain has sweetened the air and left the sidewalks littered with lilac blossoms that stick to Ida's blue sneakers, startling her continually with their brightness. She paces the neighborhood. Five blocks west, one to the north. The houses along her chosen route are all well-tended, humble houses with covered side porches, single car garages. She glimpses snatches of family life as she passes: A mother plays cards with her children; an older brother swings a smaller boy in faster and faster arcs, then sets the boy on the grass to stagger giddily. She thinks of the Queen of the Farfans, how if she were here instead of Ida, she would be surrounded by family. What's more, she would be suffused with a sustaining faith, the kind that lets you eat substandard damaged food with gratitude, the kind that generates grace. The Queen of the

Farfans would be beloved and honored in the midst of her sprawling, improvised family. She would not be scuffing along alone, rebuffed, a yearning voyeur.

Faith, oh faith—Ida felt she'd lost every last shred of it. And hers had been such a simple one. Not for her the holy mysteries, the binding sorrow, the flashing sword of retribution. Not for her the hardened jaw, the blast of hate masquerading as righteousness. It was Mary, the Mother, she's been drawn to, not the pious Son or the fire-breathing Father. Her sole and abiding belief had been in her family, her roles as Jack's wife and Dave's mother. Sacrifice? Willing suspension of belief? Oh, don't get her started. But then Ida's family, that tiny, fragile unit, had up and left her, and now she was, she realized, just like any other disillusioned soul aching from the pronounced hole in her center.

On Cadwalder Avenue, just as Ida slows again to dab at her eyes, Chuck, the Finnertys' new dog, appears from behind a severely pruned laurel hedge and falls in step beside her. Ida gives him a sidelong look, sighs, and pockets her tissue.

"C'mere, you," she says, scooping the dog into her arms. She removes the little girl's undershirt twisted around his belly while he breathes heavily. As she places him back down on the sidewalk, he thanks her by licking her hand.

"All right, then," she instructs him, "go home now, Lil' Bit. Flee those crazy girls."

The dog, a stocky terrier, tilts his head in genuine consideration before continuing alongside Ida. Chuck seems to know exactly where he is going. He pads through the still intersections without a glance to either side, making Ida feel almost foolish when she casts obligatory looks right and left. Before long, he's led her back to her own street. The mailman is just leaving her house when Ida and Chuck round the corner together. And on his heels is Cloris, with a new pixie haircut, tucking her hand inside Ida's mailbox. Ida slows, then ducks behind the big sycamore on the corner. Chuck pauses also, nonchalantly sniffing the back of the tree as if the delay is his own idea. When Ida glances at her porch again, Cloris is clambering over her porch rail, heading towards the backyard.

"Isn't *that* interesting?" Ida makes a face at Chuck. They've barely reached the porch themselves—Ida's own hand in her mailbox—when she hears the phone ring.

"Well, mystery solved," Joanie says, flatly. "Farfan's selling exotic cars in Silver City, Nevada. He'd always wanted to go west, he said."

"What about his mission, the autoharp, the Queen?"

" 'I'm done with all that,' Farfan told investigators. Apparently, his new religion is rare Italian roadsters—Isotta Fraschinis, Bugattis—false icons, if you ask me," Joanie hoots. "At least the Queen is vindicated."

"And she's still got the girls," Ida adds.

It isn't until a half-hour later, after combing over every last Farfan detail with Joanie, that Ida finally hangs up the kitchen phone. Chuck is leaning companionably on her right foot, his head tilted upwards in her direction. He observes as she reaches into her pocket for one of her tiny Sub-Rite cigarettes and spreads the mail out over the counter. The same old circulars. The old people catalogues: health aids and mail order pre-cooked food. And, then, stuck against the electric bill, a lumpy pink envelope addressed, this time, to Ida. No sketches or stickers grace the outside of this envelope. Inside, Ida finds a tiny dog biscuit and a hand-drawn Mother's Day card featuring a taller version of one of Cloris's almond-eyed girls. She wears oversize glasses like Ida's, and her flipped up silvery hair is embedded with a spiky blue and gold crown. Beside her high-heeled foot perches a shaggy creature with enormous pointed ears and a fierce toothy grin and behind them is a ring of girls all holding hands, grinning to beat the band.

< 148 >

*I'm losing it*, Ida thinks, because now she really does hear a band. Well, music, at least, and it's coming from her backyard. She's actually relieved to see the Finnerty girls are back and practicing the May Procession.

It takes Ida only a moment to recognize the garments that adorn the girls. Cloris has gotten into her closet, and she and her sisters are dazzling. Here is Hattie, tripping around in Ida's favorite shirtwaist, a dress she has not fit into for at least two decades, a sky blue and pink plaid with a fabric-covered belt and cloth buttons. Ida can remember wearing that dress the day she walked Dave to first grade, delivering him to Sister Mariella. He'd tried to hold her back for a moment, his fingers laced through that fancy belt. At least she thought that's what he'd been doing, but when she bent to reassure him and release his grip, Dave, excited, had whispered loudly into her ear: "You're the prettiest mommy here."

And Ellie! Would you get a load of Ellie, Ida could hear Jack saying. The girl might be all of twenty-five years old, posing elegantly in Ida's beaded black cocktail dress. Even the hem dragging on the grass seems devil-may-care. Only her bare muddy toes, poking out of a glitzy pair of silver, high-heeled sandals, give Ellie away as a child. And yet they too recall the past, nights when neither she nor Jack could wait, when they giggled their way to the back garden and her pantyhose ended up behind the brick barbecue. Ida shakes her head, but she can't stop smiling.

They've perched Jemma statue-like on Ida's patio table and draped her in a blue shawl Ida wore to a picnic once. The picnic had promised to be something of a disaster; it had been her retirement celebration, and great thunderheads appeared, chasing the party indoors. But even with thunder and lightning, a hammering rain flailing the host's concrete patio, the men—including a patient version of Jack and a surprisingly jocular Dave—grandly continued barbecuing. Wet to the skin, they flourished their spatulas and drank beers and loudly traded jokes between the thunderclaps and downpours. The hamburgers and hot dogs they delivered in the oddly soaked and toasted buns tasted more delicious than any she could remember. What a party that had been! Had she ever laughed so much?

Ida can't help herself; she laughs aloud now. She's tickled to pieces by all these versions of her life—until Cloris enters her line of vision, Cloris, carrying a crown of twisted lilac on a damp green cushion from the patio chair set as if it were Ida's tea tray. *By all rights*, Ida thinks, *the girl should be in my wedding gown*, but instead Cloris is wearing Ida's own favorite outfit, her long blue sweater with the sagging patch pockets, her favorite worn corduroys, her own canvas gardening shoes. The sight unaccountably touches Ida, as do the Finnertys' high, fluting voices as they pour their hearts into the second verse:

*Our voices ascending*
*In harmony blending*
*Oh thus may our hearts turn*
*Dear Mother to Thee.*

Ida has to turn away. She wipes her eyes and then, to steady herself, slips Chuck the biscuit and, while he crunches appreciatively, bends to show him the card. She doesn't point out that the two rows of cancelled stamps on the envelope, undeniably French, are secondhand and have been stuck across the corner of the envelope with crisscross pieces of cellophane tape. Nor does she note aloud the familiar childish scrawl and the absence of a postmark.

"That's you," she tells the dog, tapping on his portrait.

As the girls reach the patio and another round of the chorus— *Queeeeen of the Angels, Queeeeen of the May*—Cloris pauses before the glass doors and smiles gravely at Ida, who is wearing her old familiar smile again as she crouches beside the attentive dog.

"And this," she is saying, stroking the crown decking the card's main figure, a clear object of adoration, "...well, this...Chuck, this must be Madame Ida."

# TEMPTATION OF THE TUTELARY

We were all envious of T'ang. Such continuous, glorious trouble. The fellow never fully rested, always catching the slovenly shirttails of his hell-bent Incarnate, whispering in her ear, shoving pillows into place, somersaulting through space to snatch away keys and little hillocks of cocaine and hide them in plain sight. Fun, fun, fun. Meanwhile, our own Incarnates, all residents of the Gilded Age Villa, gave only the illusion of movement. The lamentable Mary Wilson might not even have approached that dubious vibrancy, which is to say you couldn't entirely fault PlainField for what was to come.

You have to stick with the one you've got, for better or for worse. And it was the latter that brought us all to the Villa. We had spent predictable years with our Incarnates, safeguarding souls and preventing physical mishaps, and we all agreed the Early Years were the best, full of drama, a constant dance of near-misses: coins stolen from cloakroom closets, chased balls and speeding traffic, open poison within reach, electrical sockets, pedophiles, glass-strewn lots. The real heart-shorn grunt decisions to lie and cheat and steal. And the next stage, too... anything but boring—cars, cars, heavenly cars *and* sex, a liquor bottle jostling in a brown paper bag, sex, drugs, and sex. Who hasn't managed a stunning save at that point? But after that, good lord (excuse the expression), how the days begin to drag. The least patient of us has made no bones about losing interest.

Like the Villa residents, we are a mix, the majority coming from the Turning Generation, a smattering of Mid-Centurians, another group representing the Floundering Stage, and, of course, T'ang with his New Arrival. Others drift through, attached to the Help, but the Villa's pay is so paltry no one but Nurse Eleanor and Fat Thalia stick around. Nonetheless, yes, yes, all of us rightly could be called Guardian Angels, a term not one of us remaining has ever cared for.

Let me be clear: We stand outside doctrine—unofficially acknowledged tutelary spirits. Yet who could imagine a mortal world without us? We are Saint Anthony, unearthing the misplaced; Saint Jude, uncocking the gun in the mouth. We are *one's better nature* and *intuition*, ever unheralded and misunderstood. And we have been content to be uncomplaining proof, if you will, of God's grace, that enduring puzzle.

Until PlainField, that is. Until PlainField scotched the wicket, upset the apple cart, screwed the pooch. Until PlainField, made both oblivious and desperate by the crushing boredom of his assignment, burst through in a show of disobedience that brought up bad memories for everyone involved, even those who had foresworn the very habit of remembering.

———————

The trouble began with the arrival of Constance, a kitchen worker. Constance: a ripe seventeen-year-old, churlish, greedy, and improvident to the extreme. Kitchen workers come and go, come and go, as if through the proverbial swinging kitchen door—though doors at the Gilded Age snap shut with high, illogical latches and are, more often than not, entered by means of a coded electronic keypad.

I can't say any of us noticed the moment of Constance's arrival, which occurred during yet one more naptime in yet one more day blanketed with naptimes. The air, tainted with the noontime stench of a reconstituted lamb stew, had all but congealed, and the lack of oxygen put the residents to sleep. Most of us nodded, too, as best we could (*and why not?*), and likely wouldn't have noticed Constance or T'ang until well after dinner if not for PlainField and his endless rant.

Oh, PlainField. He'd once been magnificent, truly. Those of us who knew him in earlier circles could recall a great churning presence, grandly pearlescent, with an irresistible scent of heady myrrh and a mesmerizing, subterranean hum of the kind that emanated from purple moors and windswept, moonlit beaches. He'd shrunk more than a bit during his sojourn with Mary Wilson, grown gray and frayed, the hum more of a low-level whine. That marvelous scent had worn away, too, replaced with a medicinal sourness not unlike a mustard plaster that intensified with his frustration.

That day, PlainField had been pacing as usual, absently rearranging the line of abandoned walkers and wheelchairs, wheels straight, backs against the wall. Even furious, he exuded order. And he was vexed to high heaven. Mary Wilson's false teeth were loose, and PlainField had lurked around the luncheon table waiting for her to choke, a minor, self-defeating call to industry, but a call nonetheless. The trouble was that, despite her lack of discernible wits, the old girl had foregone all but the softest foods. As in all things, pablum was her pleasure, and she spooned in applesauce and whipped potatoes and artificially sweetened butterscotch pudding with the seriousness of a television food critic. To top off that frustration, the night before, Mary Wilson had experienced another slight stroke in her sleep, an event that had wiped clean the last twinkling synapse ruling her simple moral sphere. In other words, she didn't give a damn any longer about right and wrong. Any lingering consideration as to whether or not to filch her tablemates' pudding had vanished—*pfff...ttt!*—and horribly, this too had taken PlainField by surprise.

The greatest tragedy was that, for all Mary Wilson's lapses, for all her mental foibles and ambulatory weakness, she possessed the heart and lungs of a young woman. Her doctor had declared as much just last week, oblivious to the vibrating moaning that rattled the corner of the examination room where PlainField wept.

So, on the unfortunate afternoon of Constance's arrival, none of us doubted that PlainField's pacing would be mere prelude to a roar. He began by arguing—oh, how fruitless; it wearied us no end—with the heavens. His usual complaints were reason-centered. *Given X, why Y? Why this? Why that?* That day, he'd forgone his usual exercises in failed logic. A new fury bit his sepulchral bones: names—*our names*.

Those who came before us, PlainField professed, had been given appellations of affection and familiarity, names that would become legend: *Raphael, Uriel, Michael ("He Who Is as God")*. With nomenclature like that—*He Who Is as God!*—the task was clear: guard the souls of men. From whence, then, had arrived the Misconception, the Great Shift that shook us from the safekeeping of souls to the fuss and bluster of pulling a sad-sack businessman back from a busy curb in a foreign city?

"C'mon now," PlainField argued, "who amongst us ever believed in unintentionality?"

And here was the deeper cut: Plainfield's realization about the way He'd had some fun with our generation, naming us after the humdrum: geographical markings, commonplace items, even (as in PlainField's case) after the very housing developments our Incarnates would eventually occupy. Among the most senior of us were Key-Stone, WaterMark, MainLand, BlisterPack, CrossRoads, DeerRun. A terrible joke, it would appear. One might even say it verged on being cruel. Our contingent had been followed by a slight turn toward lyricism: FloatingBeetle, LiltingBridge, BlueMoon. Not so dramatic a shift, really, but the improvement seemed a torturous elevation to PlainField. And now he was chafing at a recent rumor that the newest generations had been christened after kingdoms.

I'll be frank: rants toward Heaven rattle even the most complacent of us. The memories of our Incarnates might be fractured and irretrievable, but ours are twined within us, and our very beings proclaim that no lasting good comes from insurrection. With a slight shared glance, we rallied that afternoon. Adjustments were made, and PlainField was conveniently interrupted by a somnambulant parade toward the television room and yet another viewing of *It's a Wonderful Life.* PlainField turned his wrath toward Hollywood. While he seethed, Mary Wilson slumped, open-mouthed, in her favorite armchair in front of the constant replay of that infuriating Jimmy Stewart, wavering on the bridge.

"Jump! Jump!" PlainField sang out.

We couldn't fault him, exactly. All of us hoped to be on such a bridge one day, and none of us would ever sink so low as to invent that angel's ridiculous tale. Time and again, PlainField ruined the movie for any semi-lucid soul by ringing bells right and left as Jimmy Stewart wavered. We were settling back, relieved that PlainField's rant had burned down to a single shake of his head as he uttered one last rueful, "Kingdoms," when a spate of giggling reached us, and we noticed we'd been joined by a newcomer, an elegant young swain sprawled across the linoleum hallway.

"It's *dynasties*, actually," he drawled, "not..."

He interrupted his statement to rise in a gorgeous flutter of white and golden luminosity, the like of which we had not seen in some time, to dash to the dining room. There, he gracefully intercepted a tray of cascading soup bowls, preventing the lot from landing on the head of a slovenly teenager none of us recognized.

"...not *kingdoms*," he continued, returning. "As in Semerkhet and Qa'a, Sanakht and Djoser, Han, Qin, Xia, and Zhou." He finished, "I am T'ang."

"Like the astronaut juice?" asked PlainField with undisguised hope.

T'ang smiled. "The cultural zenith of Imperial China, actually."

"Lovely," said KeyStone, insensitive to PlainField's frown. "And who is *that*?" He motioned toward the girl in the dining room, now assiduously applying hand sanitizer to her hands and wrists and forearms as if it were bug repellent.

"Oh, *that*," T'ang said, wrinkling his pretty brow. "*That* is my own dear cross to bear: Miss Constance Solnicki."

If any of us had been looking at PlainField at that moment, we might have seen the whole tragic play ahead. As it was, a guttural sound escaped his lips, and we turned in time to catch a glimpse of his anguished desire, which, to be candid, we all shared.

"*Constance*," PlainField murmured.

"Ah, yes, Constance, Connie," T'ang said. "Cunnie Bunnie, the dear heart, the little scamp."

He'd barely gotten out the words when a bundle of fluted paper pill cups tipped floorward. As Nurse Eleanor bent to retrieve them, one of Constance's pale, nicotine-stained hands shot out in what certainly seemed like a well-practiced motion. She might have succeeded—she surely would have snagged at least the nearest fluted cup, the one filled with Everett Dubie's Haldol—if not for T'ang. Talk about well-practiced! His resigned shove sent the cart past Nurse Eleanor and out of Constance's reach.

"I'm getting clumsy in my old age." Nurse Eleanor actually apologized to the girl, who stood to one side, biting a cuticle in irritation while her other hand played absently with a loose cigarette in her pocket. We all felt a stirring inside, our ethereal appendages scrambling in our own pockets.

"She shouldn't smoke. She's pregnant, of course," T'ang sighed.

"And...," Plainfield said.

"She doesn't have a clue. Not consciously, at least. Two weeks in."

"Tell us more," PlainField begged, his eyes following Constance. "The father?"

"Impossible," T'ang said. "Motorcycles, drugs, abject madness."

"Ha!" A cackle escaped one of our group.

"Guns," he added, wearily, enticingly. "A gang. Communicable diseases. Cockfights."

Thalia, the kitchen manager, hugely obese and slow-moving, was toddling over to claim Constance for dinner-prep training. We all noticed the way Constance took note of the keys at Nurse Eleanor's waist even as she reluctantly left the meds tray behind to stumble through three desultory tries at the keypad before opening the kitchen door. T'ang didn't move. He sprawled over the loveseat by the corner window and yawned extravagantly.

"Shouldn't you...?" WaterMark, a master fretter from way back, began. "I mean"—he batted a wing in our direction—"shouldn't he...I mean, she needs...well, don't you think?"

That last was uttered in such a plaintive tone that we all laughed a bit too giddily. It had been so long. All but PlainField. He had grown considerably, unfurling himself from the hunched, pacing apparition he'd been earlier into a more recognizable shadow of his grander self.

T'ang, unmoved by WaterMark's anxiety, our merriment, or PlainField's agitation, yawned again, and the very air around us trembled with new energy. "You can't imagine how tiring...," he said, as if continuing another conversation. His enormous eyes inched shut, and his brilliance dimmed, even as a crash from the kitchen set us all upright.

"I'll go," PlainField volunteered.

"Not possible," we chided. "You know that."

< 158 >

"Just the once," he pleaded.

Only as Companion, only as Observer, we cautioned, our own eyes skittering to the recalcitrant T'ang, who was slowly glimmering back. Before we could warn him, just like that, he'd vanished, with PlainField trailing after him, a renewed radiance in his wake. We might have all followed them, but truthfully our own languor was too pronounced. We did what we'd become best at. We waited.

———————————

Constance served at dinner that night without direct incident, though anyone paying the slightest attention noticed the special care she took with one of Mary Wilson's two dinner partners, Miss Jeannie. Although shrunken and pleasantly absent now, Miss Jeannie had been a pistol (ask KeyStone!) in her youth and sported the jewels to show for it. Every finger encrusted with gems, the real thing. Constance couldn't take her eyes off the old woman's hands, and we held our collective breath as she knelt to pick up Miss Jeannie's fallen napkin and tuck in back on her lap.

"Did she?" KeyStone asked, a simpleton-like joy lighting his face.

We nodded, having seen Constance's practiced move, the ruby-and-diamond ring slipping off the old worn knob onto the more supple one, then—flash!—into the front pocket of Constance's newly assigned Mother Hubbard apron.

"Oh, T'aaaang," PlainField called out.

The air tingled, but T'ang affected not to hear.

"Now, don't get excited," LiltingBridge yawned. "She'll be found out. Summoned and dismissed. They all get caught eventually. My girl Thalia's already on it."

LiltingBridge had a point. Fat Thalia may not have looked quick, but she missed nothing. There's good reason she'd survived so long at Gilded Age. Her heavy-lidded eyes had caught the swish of napkin, Constance's alacrity in retrieving it, the lingering sway around Miss Jeannie. Thalia's left eyebrow was rising, a sure sign.

T'ang, the beautiful one, only snorted, a sound that resembled nothing so much as a fluted horn. We needn't have wondered at his insouciance. Because, oh that Constance. She'd felt Thalia's attention before LiltingBridge, even—or so it seemed. Just as Thalia set a last dish upon the table and prepared to whisk the new girl off by her elbow for an inspection, Constance bent to cut Miss Jeannie's meat, and when she straightened up again, the ring had miraculously reappeared on the old woman's finger.

KeyStone and WaterMark clapped aloud. It was such a lovely move, really. Only LiltingBridge appeared not to appreciate its grace.

"She's a pro," T'ang said.

"Oh, yes," PlainField crooned. "Oh, yes."

What a dance the next few days would be! Constance's cleverness always on show. And, even PlainField, wherever he's gone, would have to admit that T'ang was masterful as well, with a calculating ease to his interventions. Yes, they were a well-matched couple indeed.

---

Couples were rare in the Villa, but Doris Hellinger and Taddy Brink were a Villa item. In their former lives, their paths would not have crossed, and even if they had, it was unlikely the two would have noticed each other. At a dinner party, they might even have been set far apart to secure the serenity of the evening. Taddy, a near-famous physicist, an agnostic, a lover of terse, cutting pronouncements and adroit practical jokes involving weak lasers and live animals. Taddy, a cruel man, really, enraptured only by mental brilliance and the private well of scientific inquiry, a misogynist and loner, despite his enduring union to a gentle woman who had not understood the contract she'd

< 160 >

signed when marrying a genius. And Doris, a railing widow, she of
the Republican Women's Club, of the Christian Women's League,
of school-board battles and cocktail-party feuds. Doris, who could
not string together a meaningful sentence on paper, but commanded
rooms with her nonstop brassy voice, always several decibels louder
than anyone else's. Yes, in their former, memory-driven lives, these
two might have come to physical blows. In dementia's grip, however,
Taddy and Doris had unraveled into a couple of agreeable people who
seemed to believe they were seated on adjoining bar stools, continu-
ing a years-long flirtation. They'd each recognized the beany, steel
core of the other. They did not know how or why, and truly, it did
not matter. That recognition was everything. It contented them both.

For most of each morning, they slept, side by side, in matching
wing chairs at the end of the hall. When cajoled, they shuffled to the
television room to derail the "Pass the Beach Ball" exercise by tossing
the ball only toward each other. Doris sometimes napped in Taddy's
bed, wrapped within a multi-pocketed gray sweater that engulfed her
dwindled frame, while Taddy dozed on the blue corduroy recliner his
real wife had installed in his private room. Only at meals did they
willingly separate, the staff seating Taddy with "the Boys"—the Villa's
other three men—while little hump-backed Doris slumped inches
away at a table with the amiable Miss Jeannie and the ever-vacant
Mary Wilson.

On the Sundays Taddy's wife visited, she pulled him to his feet
and away from Doris, marching him back to his room to dress him in
clothes she liked better than the gravy-stained pink Madras sports coat
and gray velour sweatpants he preferred. Once she'd spiffed up Taddy
in a fresh outfit—the few white hairs on his mottled pate smoothed
down, the bristle on his cheeks removed—she would settle him in the
recliner with a needless afghan over his knees and page through the
three photograph albums she kept on his nightstand. Like an endless

< 161 >

night of vacation slides with the neighbors, her relentless commentary revolved around detailed descriptions of people and events that meant absolutely nothing to Taddy. But good-hearted stranger that he'd become, he nodded at the woman beside him and occasionally even managed a brief expression that lay somewhere between a grin and the face he made while straining on the toilet.

Tuesdays and Thursdays, rain or shine, Doris's daughter stiff-walked her mother out into the fortressed garden, where they'd perch on a bench and share a couple of cigarettes, with the daughter showing Doris (again) how to flick the silver lighter she was forbidden to possess at the Villa and which never failed to delight her. All the old ladies retained a love for the wiggle and dance of a high blue flame. After a half-hour or so, the daughter—no youngster herself—would reclaim the lighter, fluff up her mother's hair, maneuver her back to the hall chair beside Taddy, and run down the carpeted hall before Doris could repeat and repeat her usual question about the door code. Though Doris had mislaid many desires, she'd kept this recently acquired one—her desperate wish to open that door—and she'd often lurch behind her daughter's fleeing figure, calling out, "Miss? Oh, Miss?" until Taddy, insensible to nearly everything else, raised his head and tapped his cane to bring her back. We were barely roused. The exchange was, like every other here, sadly predictable.

———

Two weeks in and Constance was an old-timer. When a round of flu depleted the staff, she was promoted out of the kitchen and into laundry and room servicing. The promotion was, we could all see, a boon for Constance, who hovered daily around the room Mary Wilson shared with Miss Jeannie. And a greater boost for PlainField, who, bound to follow Mary Wilson, was for once thankful for this duty.

With Constance's promotion came one significant difficulty: She could no longer duck out the kitchen door for a smoke. Her breaks were far more regulated and never long enough. She was queasy—we could see that—with slight waves of morning sickness she attributed to a need for nicotine, and bright girl that she was, Constance soon discovered her best chance of an on-the-job smoke came on those glorious mornings when Doris's daughter would eagerly share cigarettes in return for help killing time with Doris. Sometimes, the daughter would even skip out early, avoiding that scene with the locked door, leaving Constance minding Doris with a second round of cigarettes. Even T'ang relaxed then. After all, Doris possessed nothing worth a con.

Yet PlainField remained vigilant. Longing did him good. We could all see that. His cheeks were rosy again, his air incandescent rather than ashen.

"Switch for just one night," he pestered T'ang. "Look how nicely she's settling in. Really, it would be mere babysitting. And you could rest with Mary Wilson."

"An interlude," he insisted. "Nothing more."

"It is forbidden." T'ang yawned. "So sorry."

Who was tempting whom here? We observed, unsure. We too had been seduced by Constance Solnicki and her slatternly drama, her barroom fetor of stale beer and cigarettes so crushingly welcome in the Villa's artificial freshness. We all had eyes for her, our envy of T'ang heating up by the day. But do not assume we did nothing. We did try to awaken PlainField and T'ang by conjuring reminders of the enduring temptations He suffered in His forty days and forty nights in the desert.

LiltingBridge replaced dinner rolls with stones.

DeerRun fell headlong off the higher ledges, the plastic crown moldings, in the Family Room—and not one of us raced to catch him.

BlueMoon reconfigured the television so that instead of showing black-and-white comedies, *All the President's Men*, that morality play of greed and hubris, played in a constant loop.

Testing faith, we tried to illustrate to PlainField, was an ever-fruitless endeavor, and craving power even more disastrous.

T'ang seemed amused by our charades. PlainField flat did not notice. Intent on flexing his skills, he shadowed Constance, waiting for his chance to intervene. Poor T'ang now had two responsibilities, and we must admit he juggled them admirably. In hindsight, perhaps it might have been better if T'ang had succumbed. An intervention might have appeared, their own better natures arriving like a heavenly cavalry. Instead, PlainField read T'ang's reaction as a challenge, not resistance, and eventually he crossed a line. As Constance lingered in the windless garden with Doris, finishing the daughter's last two cigarettes and preening a little over the acquisition of the engraved silver lighter, forgotten in the daughter's escape, PlainField rushed in with a demonstration, a psychic slap on the hand, a gesture just large enough to jar her better nature and sidestep a theft.

"Oh, dear," DeerRun muttered, pointing unnecessarily.

But PlainField had gone to work. He rattled the fence gate with unholy force, and a cascade of leaves whirled up the swept path, rushing at Constance. For the briefest moment, an image of hooded figures crowded the path, and Constance, who'd been about to pocket the engraved silver lighter—Constance, that pro—instinctively bailed, shoving the lighter into a pocket of Doris's tent-like sweater and holding up her empty hands to an even emptier pathway.

That evening at dinner, Taddy sucked down a prune, choking to death as quietly and pleasantly as he did everything these days. Little gullops of breath, each one smaller and more ineffectual than the other. A matter of seconds really before his head fell to his chest. T'ang, bless him, noticed it first, and soon LiltingBridge had whispered into Fat Thalia's ear and Nurse Eleanor was summoned. The hubbub caused Doris Hellinger to raise her eyes from her own prunes in time to see her Taddy being carted off by women she did not recognize, and she fought away from the table.

"Now, Doris," Thalia tried to soothe her. "You come wait here." They were the same words she used to distract Doris from Taddy's wife. A disgruntled Doris acquiesced, shivering as she reconciled herself to staring at Taddy's empty chair. In her haste to leave the table, she had thrown off her old gray sweater. Who noticed as tissues and bobby pins spilled from the sweatered pockets, a messy nest that landed right in Mary Wilson's lap? Not PlainField. He even missed the unfamiliar flare of curiosity that crossed Mary Wilson's features as her blind fingers inched through this unforeseen gift to reach around the silver lighter.

Constance was on the move. What efficiency. Like the crisp snap of hospital corners on the sheets, our Constance was a wonder to behold. She followed every protocol, foremost of all guiding the residents, who must be shielded from Death, back to their rooms—with one exception. She led Doris and Mary Wilson and Miss Jeannie into Doris's private room, settling them on the bed like a trio of old dolls. Constance was in and out in thirty seconds, locking the door behind her—protocol again.

And then she was off! Could you blame any of us, our charges safely stored away, for wanting to witness the finale? PlainField—we could see from our places on the ethereal bleachers—was gearing up for a save even as Miss Jeannie's jewelry boxes were ransacked, but he was too enthralled for the moment to take action. Even T'ang hesitated when, pockets filled with booty, Constance fled down the emptied corridors toward the locked kitchen door and for once expertly punched in the code.

"T'ang," we whispered.

"PlainField," we sighed.

The fresh air of chaos had invaded the Villa, and we all momentarily rejoiced, not noticing how Mary Wilson struggled a moment or two before Miss Jeannie, a practiced hand with a lighter, stepped right in. Nor did any of us observe how, together, joyfully, they decorated Doris's room, one candled lick at a time.

When the smoke alarms went off, we were shocked to find ourselves in the Villa kitchen with Constance, a mere breath behind PlainField and T'ang. Far too much time was spent sniffing around kitchen burners before sprinklers went off in earnest and awareness descended.

Too late. Too late. *God help us all.*

Fires surged, and we did nothing as Constance galloped to the employee lot where, miracle of miracles, her salt-pocked Gremlin started on the first try. Even PlainField seemed stunned by the speed in which she vanished. Gone, gone, gone. Did T'ang look back? I sincerely doubt it.

The rest of us had no choice. Either cowed or delighted, our Incarnates were stupefied, riveted. Smoke surrounded them, poured through them, as if they'd already ascended, becoming with each plumy explosion more shadow, less substance. With little yelps, we could feel the bonds release, one by one by one, and still even PlainField lingered. It seemed that Constance had made devils out of all of us, because here, finally, we were free to go, and yet for the longest time not one was willing to relinquish a place within the illuminated calamity she'd left behind. It was as if our Constance left an entire glowing soul with us, and in those final moments we each rushed to claim a blazing piece and burst into life at last.

## A DEAD MAN'S LAND

Dom had been just shy of three years old when Sven brought him to us, a smidgen of a being already saddled with a clouded past. No young mother in tow, only that brash father with his heavy pockets, tearing through the county as if bearing a heat-seeking map. The pair, who arrived in a late-model car so shiny it looked as if it had been waxed every mile, might have landed from the moon, they seemed so insensible of ordinary protocol. It was noted, for instance, how the toddler boy perched without restraint on the milky leather upholstery, his mitten hands clutching the ridged dashboard, the father oblivious to danger. How far had they traveled like this? No one knew, and if anyone did inquire, say, a smitten shopgirl, Sven would look right past her, pausing long enough to make her remember and regret every awkward moment of her life.

At the town's single hotel, once-elegant, still genteel, the bellhop noted hardly any luggage in the trunk, and when he went to park the car, he was struck by the vehicle's cleanliness, the lack of even a gum wrapper, a faint metallic odor its only noticeable stain. The child possessed no visible toys, no soft scrap of coddled flannel. His father, it seemed, was his sole diversion and comfort. Although Sven barely returned the attention, the boy followed him, imitating as best he could that long confident stride, and as the child tired, *before* he tired, the young father—barely more than a boy himself—would lift the child absentmindedly onto his hip, and Dom would turn his face toward Sven's tight shoulder as if embarrassed at having to succumb to sleep so publicly, so helplessly.

< 167 >

The land Sven pursued was part of a place local Choctaws once called *Nahopalah* or *Nahopoa laha*, the name translating loosely to "marked by the beast," a label white settlers believed indicated prime hunting grounds. Those settlers had lusted after the land as much as Sven and fabricated claims. They'd booted out the Indians as soon as they could, only to discover a dearth of game on that pristine acreage. Such disappointment. But not one of them ready to suggest they give it back. They had principles, hadn't they? Trumpeting desires?

Over time, the land had been divided among three ordinary white families. Those families farmed a bit and raised fancy-wooled sheep, Cotswolds and Karakuls, and considered themselves the town cream. When Sven began to nose around, making shallow, insinuating offers, they laughed him off at first. Then out of necessity—the man would not relent—they brought out guns and dogs and threats. A normal man would have fled or at the least scaled down his hopes and retreated to another part of the county. Not Sven. He hovered in town, practicing his steely dimples on flustered bankers as he patiently awaited a shift. Almost on cue, the neighboring families began to fall apart: Krueger got the cancer; Milton's eldest, never handy, had that accident with a chainsaw; Sanderslon's wife ran off with her own brother. Yes, one by one, the old families succumbed to ruin and madness, and soon Dom's cocky young father presided over an overgrown paradise of field and meadow and tangled hardwood forest fused with that old bad luck. Only a fool would trespass after that. Nineteen years later, the glorious parcel would still be called Dead Man's Land, a name the nearly grown Dom would relay to a little girl without a shred of irony during the afternoon Sven himself was buried.

---

< 168 >

"But it is a dead man's land *now*, isn't it?" the little girl asked Dom, pleased with her own cleverness.

She was Sven's niece, a relation previously unknown to Dom, arrived with her parents for the funeral. The little girl in her Sunday skirt and Dom still in his bereavement suit had just crossed the edge of the notorious woods and were wading through a dappled clearing strewn with bird-foot violet.

"Actually, no," Dom said. "It's mine now. And I ain't dead yet, am I?"

"Nope, not yet," the little girl offering a smirk that stung with familiarity.

It had been Dom's idea, sparked and sudden, to take this new cousin on a tour of the land, and an observer might be forgiven for seeing a lovely synchronicity to his invitation: Dom, the new heir, ushering another child along the property edges the way Sven had once led him. Back then Sven had used toddler Dom as mere audience, witness to a triumph the boy wouldn't fully understand or care about for years. A dog might have served the same purpose. The greedy-eyed girl was another story. She vibrated with an intemperate hunger Dom well recognized.

*She's out to find trouble*, he thought. *Well, then.*

"We'll go through a forest," Dom had promised her back at the farmhouse, "straight into a secret world."

"Secret," she scoffed, but her tiny, pointed eyebrows had raised, and barely suppressing a jig, she accepted his outstretched hand and let him lead her away from the post-funeral giddiness into the bristled honeyed fields behind Sven's house.

The bird-foot violet behind them, they reached a hedge of snowberry bushes.

Masses of them. A cloud on a hill. The girl darted forward to finger the white berries, but Dom tugged her along, the tiny hand surprisingly rough in his palm.

"C'mon now," he called over his shoulder as she half-tumbled behind him down a steep pebbled path. "This is what you wanted, isn't it?"

A breeze rose and sharpened, wailing. They followed the path to a stream and then followed the stream into a rock tunnel and out again where the gem of Dom's inheritance lay, a hidden lagoon surrounded by high rock walls and a stretch of yellow sand beach. A place so private not even birdsong breeched the silence.

"It *is* secret," the little girl gloated, sassy again. "It's my secret place."

Dom might have corrected her. Mine, he could have said, not yours. But she would find out soon enough, he reckoned, how deep his fortunes ran.

---

What Dom had owned: nothing, nothing, not one damned thing. He'd roamed through childhood like an animal, a creature without knowledge of pockets or locked doors. Sven might have believed that his son's needs remained simple, any ambition craven and unformed. Still, on the day he'd come into his majority, Dom had been consumed by an unreasonable excitement, half-expecting his father to deed him a bit of the woods or even present him with his first steady allowance, a token for twenty-one years of filial servitude. So silly. Of course, Sven had let the day elapse without a nod.

Dom had been stunned by his own reaction. A blistering fury rushed through him, blued his vision, hazed the light. For hours, he could not see straight. He banged out of the house and spent the light of his birthday flailing through a forest raked with sudden, violent winds, limbs cracking around him as he cursed the land that should be his and the father that kept it from him. Was he worth nothing? Had he no birthright? Dom knew better.

Any other young man surely would have confronted Sven, had it out with him with smashed-up walls and bloodied fists, and perhaps Dom would have as well, if Sven's own illness, virulent and deadly swift, had not appeared almost the next day as if a rebuke to the man's selfishness. Or a wish. Yes, sure, Sven's illness seemed to arrive as a granted wish, as if the entire town had drawn a communal winning lottery ticket. Dom knew no one would be challenging that bequest. Only the most recent girlfriend mourned Sven, but as townspeople told each other, that gal had known him less than two months, and most of those weeks he'd spent near-mute, dying. Who wouldn't feel something for a sweet-looking, too-young fellow dying before his time?

By then the rest of the town had long learned to see past those charmed looks. Scars and wounds, lost fortunes, nightmares crowded with ravaged daughters and white-faced, trembling sons, eviscerated pets, dawn fires, the chilling appearance of Sven at one's kitchen table, playing with knives. No, each had his own image of the man in mind, none of it attractive. If Dom's mother had been alive, well, maybe she might have ventured back at the end, not to say goodbye, God knows, but like them, to verify Sven wasn't indulging in a brutal bit of cleverness. If she'd been alive, too, perhaps she might have challenged the legacy to Dom, and if she had, they would have understood she was acting not out of greed but from concern that Sven's temperament, his very being, had soaked into the spoiled land and would contaminate Dom, her only child. A legitimate worry, they'd agree.

The man was bad luck, pure and simple. Dom's mother had spent years trying to get Sven out of her blood, and they'd heard that in the end she too had surrendered and taken up a straight razor to quicken the task.

He prepared his father's funeral alone, the girlfriend having de-camped as soon as it was clear nothing would be coming her way. She did squawk when she heard Dom's plans.

"A party," she said, disbelieving. "Are you crazy?"

He engaged a fancy caterer from forty miles away and planned a real reception to follow a memorial service and a burial smack in the center of town in the gated churchyard cemetery. As slight as her acquaintance was with Sven, the girlfriend had been shocked. Surely Dom realized how Sven would have treated his efforts. The minister certainly did. He shook throughout the brief service, waiting for the church to burst into flames as he cobbled together lies about Sven. A businessman, he called him, a citizen leader. And didn't they all hold their breath until the specks of ash and clots of dust and bone were lowered, Dom's lonely flower and that first shovelful of rocks pinging against not a casket but an old Dante cigar box tied shut with heavy twine? Released. Yes, they were released, and as they moved farther and farther away from the gravesite, in the dingiest corner of an already shaded cemetery, as they moved toward the narrow lane then out to the open parking lot, the huddle unfolded. Heads were thrown back, shoulders slapped in relief.

*Sure, sure,* they told Dom, *of course, we'll see you back at the house.*

---

Where did the others imagine Dom and the little girl had gone? To see nonexistent chickens or the goats Sven kept for target practice? Someone must have noticed their absence, because it seemed the whole town had crowded into the house. Now that the grave was secured, they had no qualms about drinking Sven's liquor and partak-ing of the endless stacks of sandwiches—truly good sandwiches—that the out-of-town caterer kept supplying: a tray of ham and cheese on

< 172 >

French baguette, roast beef and horseradish on sweet white bread, cur-
ried chicken on poppy seed rolls, and more, another tray of real pork
barbecue, smoky and fat, piled high on soft, white buns beside bowls
of vinegary slaw. A few, ever-generous souls had brought by salads and
casseroles, baskets of cookies and brownie bars, tiny berry cobblers.
The famished group—you couldn't call them mourners—couldn't get
enough. They sprawled over Sven's furniture and dirtied his china
plates; they rummaged through his cupboards for more whiskey, for
tins of imported smoked fish, for the cigars they knew Sven favored.
Soon they were checking out the medicine cabinets and bureau draw-
ers. Mementos slipped in and out of pockets. Envelopes were perused.
Fears of a curse began to shimmy away. They watched those familiar
fears fade, the furniture growing more solid, the paint on the walls
brighter. A browning houseplant in a kitchen corner revealed new
buds, a flower already opening. The house creaked uncomfortably
with snorts of real laughter. One fellow grabbed a concertina from
his car, another a fiddle.

"Good lord," whispered the stepmother of the little girl to herself.
"Will they start dancing next?"

She hadn't known Sven, they'd learned. The little girl, nine years
old, was her husband's child from an early marriage that had ended
tragically. Dom's uncle had heard of Sven's death only the day before
the service, and he and his family must have run from their house,
into car and onto plane, because they arrived twenty minutes early,
causing all manner of panic until Sven's brother, the uncle, the spitting
image, began to speak. Then they knew he wasn't Sven, come back
to life to taunt them for their brief joy. Sven's brother had a delicate,
thoughtful way about him. He admired the spill of lilies Dom had
ordered, the altar cloths, the wary neighbors themselves. He thanked
everyone for knowing Sven. Thanked them so much they were soon
certain he himself had not ever made his brother's acquaintance.

The wife was something else. She sized them all up as if drawing up ledgers in an account book, adding and subtracting potential worth, until they were all shame-faced with debt. She kept her distance, not even prowling the house with the rest of them. With an untouched plate of food on her knee, she took wincing sips of ice tea she refused to sweeten, as if it were medicine and she was on a timed regimen.

The uncle and his family were strangers to Dom as well, but when he'd found the number in Sven's desk, he'd called. Other than Dom, that brother was the last of Sven's living relations. Last "surviving," it was noted more than once. No one wondered where the brother had been all this time. If it had been any of them, you bet they would never have looked up Sven. The story was that when the brother and Sven were children, Sven had burned down the family house with his parents, two sisters, and this brother bolted within. The brother had jumped from a high window, broken both legs and a few ribs. A lung had collapsed. His hands had been badly burned. No one else survived. Sven was seven, and rocking on his heels across the street while the fire burned, he'd nursed a satisfied grin that lit his little angel face. People put it down to shock at first, then a childish accident in the early hours of dawn. Except for those who knew him. He went to live with one ill-fated foster family after another. The neighbor who took in the brother wouldn't have Sven and eventually left the state, careful to erase all possibilities of a forwarding address as she and the brother went. Sven bragged about this and bragged, too, about how he kept track of them nonetheless.

"Their every movement," he'd say, adding: "I scare the shit out of 'em."

Now here the brother was, the image of Sven, brave at last and scaring the shit out of them, arriving with his bookkeeper wife and this elfin child, Dom's only cousin, Delphine.

"Like the flower," the girl told Dom.

He shook his head. "The fish," he corrected. "Like the fish. Dolphin, it means."

She laughed, not the giggle of a child, but a full-throated appreciation. They'd hit it off right away. She caught a fly with one hand. Sven could do that, and like her, he never let the fly go, but played with it awhile. Sent outside to play with the town children, she seemed shy at first, lingering on the edges. A moment later, the high-pitched cry of an animal in distress. A taunting boy knocked from a tree, the bloodied mark of a rock blooming on his temple. The girl flitting lightly, melding into the crowd of gaping children, half of them already weeping with dread as she surveyed the land around her with a proprietary air.

*Kin*, Dom thought, *yes, she is kin.* And he knew where he needed to take her. The uncle was a different story. Mild as milk. Dom had taken an instant dislike to the uncle and his wife.

"Not my mother," the girl clarified. "Karen."

Karen, who knew every penny spent and recognized straightaway there weren't enough of them.

"Maybe he left you something," the stepmother told her husband after Dom's call. "He was your brother. He might have wanted to make amends."

After the funeral, as she sipped her bitter tea and balanced her plate, the stepmother listened and learned all that Dom had inherited. A fortune. The best land in the state. A perfect, paid-for house. The boy worked as a sales lackey in an office. He was all alone in the world. She found her husband on the back porch, surveying the well-tended garden, blood-red tomatoes bursting from an ash manure.

"My father used fish heads as fertilizer," the uncle said. "His tomatoes stopped traffic."

"You could ask," she nagged. "He has no other family."

A pair of town children giggled onto the back porch and were immediately corralled·by their mother, who lost her own smile when she saw the uncle.

"Hush," she said to the children. "A man is dead."

The uncle seemed not to hear her. His eyes were on the little girls.

"Seen Delphine?" he asked his wife.

If the girl disappeared, her stepmother would not grieve. There had been incidents—near accidents and unexplained circumstances—in which the stepmother had been steps away from lasting harm. She couldn't blame her new husband, but he seemed not to notice his daughter's moods or the newly frayed wiring or the unlikely broken step, a heavy ledge with its screws shorn away. No, the stepmother wouldn't miss the girl. Of course she had noted Delphine's absence that afternoon, but she felt safe for the moment and could not help but lie.

"A moment ago. In the kitchen, drawing pictures, eating cookies," she said.

"Eating cookies?" the uncle said. "Drawing pictures? Delphine?"

The stepmother's mouth twisted in an imitation of a smile, an idea forming.

"She likes it here," she said.

———————

The girl wanted to go swimming. She *was* a fish, she confessed without a hint of a smile. She could swim a mile underwater. No one but he had guessed that. She'd kept it a secret, even in the public pool where she'd startled the young lifeguard by swimming lap after lap underwater. She emerged a pretender, gasping although she had no need. She didn't explain all this to Dom, but eyed the trembling water of the hidden lagoon and wondered what lay beneath it, and he could tell from long experience that she was calculating how far she could convince Dom to go with her, if she could drag him to the deepest point, if he would survive. She was wearing her dance class leotard and a Sunday swirl skirt. She could swim in the leotard, no problem. Even if Dom wanted to, he wouldn't have been able to dissuade her. The expression in her eyes was all Sven's. Dom shrugged his shoulders, slipped off his shoes and socks, stripped down to his shorts. Sven had never frightened Dom. In fact, Dom might have been the only soul in the world who had made Sven both uneasy and helpless. One of Sven's more dramatic girlfriends once claimed that little Dom brought a dead dog back to life, his childish fingertips searching and searching until he pulled out all six of the bullets Sven had shot into the creature, before stroking the tangled, bloodied fur until it grew glossy and the dog began to breathe again as if sleeping off a long, carousing night. He'd left the bullets on his father's pillow.

A fantastic story, of course. Yet men in town talked about how Dom would show up at the tavern just as Sven began to ripple, the force of his anger so strong the bar top trembled. Even the owner would try to slip out the back door, already reconciled to ruin. Dom—six or eight or eleven—Dom, a rangy thirteen-year-old with oddly perfect teeth and shaggy blonde hair—would hardly need to step inside the door before Sven was on his feet and out in the parking lot, his perfectly restored truck spitting gravel against the glossy fenders and the kid left to walk home pursing that look-alike smile of Sven's. Did anyone dare offer him a ride, even out of gratitude? They did not.

Yes, such miracles were common tales, albeit unseen by most. Rumors dashed in and out of houses, through the schools and churches and the sheriff's office, but no one ever thought to share them with Dom himself. Even when he left school and might easily have peeled off a stack of Sven's bills and gone his own way, Dom stuck around as if to keep an eye on Sven. He got a job working with the local insurance agent, wore the same black suit five days a week, peddled life and major medical—terrible policies with sky-high deductibles and dismal pay-outs. Customers pitied him, but only the more desperate and foolish found themselves signing, and his commissions were few. In the evenings and on weekends, Dom minded his father's property, doing whatever chores Sven wrote down on a slip for him. Briefly, he dated a girl from the office, but she ended up marrying another fellow all in a rush and moving away overnight, it seemed.

On the surface, the water appeared almost clear, marbled with strands of variegated yellow light, but as the girl went deeper, she pushed into a relentless midnight blue. She was swimming through the night in a bottomless lagoon. Miles, she swam, hours. Finally, she neared an underwater rock cavern and saw a shimmery Dom waiting, dressed in a full black suit. As she came closer, she saw it wasn't Dom at all, but her father. No, not her father. It was the dead man, Sven; she was sure of that. Her uncle. He offered her the same measured smile he'd sent across the street as her tiny boy of a father smashed through a window and fell to the ground in a tumble of smoke and glass and flecked blood. Underwater, she chortled in fascinated recognition, that deep-throated laugh, and the laugh must have burbled its way to the surface because Dom found her then. His hands grasped her ankles, and he flung her back away from the cavern until she couldn't see a single rock, until only the slightest impression of Sven's smile remained, and even that, too, soon vanished. Such speed, such speed. She'd swum gently through the cool dark of the lagoon and now she was infuriatingly propelled, Dom's arm laid tightly across her chest. They crashed through the surface. He dragged her to the ground. Sven joined them again, a short distance away, looking as pissed off as Dom remembered from those nights he'd arrive at the tavern as if summoned.

< 178 >

"You're back," he told the girl, Delphine, as she began to breathe again on her own.

"No," she howled, feeling real anxiety for the first time in her brief life. "No, no, no." She pushed herself up on her elbows and scanned the thin, empty shore.

"No," she said again, a whisper of a wail in a little-girl voice.

"Oh, yes," Dom said. "He's gone now for good."

He recovered their twisted and tumbled clothes from behind a rock, and they dressed in a sudden hot wind, pushing damp feet into shoes and bending back into the taunting tunnel, the narrowing stream, the climb back toward the others. They would be almost dry by the time they reached the bird-foot violet again, and when they came to the house, the party would wind down all at once at the sight of Dom, the girl hardly noticed as she trudged beside him. Inside, she'd fall into Sven's recliner, looking for all the world as if she owned it, as if it owned her. She would close her eyes and plunge into a nap so deep she might have been fully drugged by the sun, the wind, the water. Dom, meanwhile, would survey the gathering, and even if no one had noticed his absence, they'd know now he was back.

It was that look of his, they reckoned later, that upended even Sven—open yet opaque, utterly guileless but knowing. Stealthily, pockets were emptied, valuables returned to drawers. Even a sandwich, wrapped in a paper napkin, meant for a quiet supper, slipped back onto a tray. The guests filed out. The caterer and her crew gathered plates, scraped and washed, and packed the van in the new silence. Dom stood on the porch and saw the whole crowd off, one by one, until only his uncle's family remained.

"Will you look at that?" the stepmother said, nudging her husband's arm and nodding toward the sleeping Delphine.

"As if she's home at last," the stepmother added. "Do you think ..." she began.

"You know," said the uncle to Dom, who'd caught every clue, "I bet Delphine would love to visit with you a while longer. Look how peaceful."

"I'll carry her for you," Dom offered and swept in before they could refuse him.

He settled her in the back seat of the uncle's car. Her eyes barely flickered, but she flinched as he moved away.

"Good luck to you," he said, holding the door open for the stepmother, who motioned again and again to the uncle with her scant black eyebrows. Say something, she implored.

"Have you nothing for me, son?" the uncle said in a low voice as he shook Dom's hand one last time, offered him a final glance at this mild version of his father's face.

Dom nearly laughed. "You don't want what I have left to give," he said, stepping away.

Anyone in town would attest to that, he knew. Certain gifts come with unbearable conditions. His uncle, of all people, should know that and be grateful to Dom, who'd set the world half-straight again. *And shouldn't they all be grateful*, Dom thought. Of course, of course, and they knew it. They did. In the coming days, wearing his single suit, Dom would take Sven's truck and visit each mourner. In the end, he'd sell more life insurance policies than he had in the last two years combined, a tiny bundle of profit all his own, the start of a whole new enterprise.

# THE NEW ARRIVAL

"They think it is impossible," she tells him, "but here is what you do. You pay a man to take your picture and make you a passport; you pay another man for stamping the passport book and yet another for a paper ticket, a sheaf of pages listing multiple destinations. You make friends with a white family. You carry their bags, discreetly hustle their little ones. You pray with them. You take a chance on a foreign god.

"It will not be easy," Frances Okonjo says, "but it won't be too difficult either. Simply move as if you were intended to move. Be as you were intended. Someone is waiting for you. Don't doubt it. Pick up your own bag (just one, neat but inexpensive), and carry it aboard. Sleep. Eat. Practice the niceties of language: please, thank you, excuse me. You *are* neat. You don't smell bad. You smell quite nice, actually. If you need to be attentive, be subtle. No googly eyes. Stay easy."

Frances Okonjo reminds him that he is not a criminal; he is a kind of refugee. A deserving refugee, one with nearly a university degree in historical geography and many useful talents. He can build anything out of nothing; he is a wizard with an oxyacetylene torch; he can bake pastry; he knows how to read weather; his touch can ease a baby's cries. "Not only that," she says, damp-eyed with admiration, "you are bearing the ultimate gift."

The city he leaves is made of red dust. It disappears behind him as if the wind generated by the taxi Frances arranged has blown it away. The city's airport, on the edge of nowhere, is nothing more than a series of corrugated metal sheds. Passengers can't observe the planes arriving or departing but must depend on a garbled public address system, the shaking of the building as a plane lands nearby, and a complicated system of shared body language, their own instincts. At some point he picks up his bag and shuffles into a line. His ticket is taken by a man with heavy glasses and a slightly soiled uniform that smells strongly of body sweat. The man worries the ticket around in his hands—back and forth—until his need becomes clear, and Frances's words are recalled: put some of your money, just a little, in a separate pocket. Peel the bills off that bundle. Some will ask; others will simply wait, and you must step in and offer. Fumbling, he manages, and finally a stub is torn off his ticket and returned to him, and then he's out on the tarmac, staggering up a metal flight of stairs against a chapping wind, bending sideways into a narrow aisle.

The woman next to him—thin, bespectacled, in an ill-fitting blue suit—falls asleep the moment she sits down. He buckles her seat belt for her. When the plane lands he climbs over her, smoothing her skirt discreetly as he passes, and retrieves his bag. She is still sleeping when he leaves, the plane emptying around her.

The next airport is a mob scene wherein he is one of many thousands. Signs flash around him; unintelligible announcements are made relentlessly. He shows his ticket and his new passport to a fat woman in a uniform, and wordlessly she jabs at a number written on the page and points him toward a steel tunnel with many small waiting rooms branching off it. At his number, he pauses and finally recognizes the name of his final destination.

Rain pours down outside, but like a child he presses himself against the glass until he can see the big jets taking off and landing. Abruptly he remembers his lessons and sits down with his book to wait. No thrillers, Frances instructed, no mysteries (why was he so interested in plotting?). She also nixed his cookbooks (why was he so interested in concoctions?) and his geography texts (why did he need to know so much about places he had—supposedly—never been?). Even his mother's Bible was rejected (nothing is more suspicious than conspicuous faith). She rooted around in his stacks of books, each one a treasure to him, and, after discarding one after another, finally approved a volume, handing it to him with a closed smile, a tight nod. "Perfect," she pronounced. He saw it was a biography of Abraham Lincoln, sixteenth president of the U.S. of A.

"A black man," Frances said, "should recognize Lincoln, and not just for his place on the American coin. An American martyr, that's what he was, the only acceptable kind."

That was a dig, he knew. She had thought better of her earlier praise, meant only to reassure him. She did not want him getting inflated ideas of his own importance.

He sits alone in the waiting room. There are no white families here. Again he joins a line. Again a stub returns to him. This time he sits next to a businessman who immediately pulls out a laptop, angling the screen away so that no one can spy. He is captivated by the way white light spills from the computer and sad when the man puts it away for takeoff and immediately captivated again when, once airborne, the businessman cracks open the laptop again and, in the darkening cabin, the white light turns blue.

He drifts off to sleep, but his empty stomach wakes him just in time for him to receive a doll-sized packet of cheese and crackers (complete with the tiniest of plastic spoons, meant, he supposes, for spreading the cheese—his little finger works just as well) and a Coca-Cola from the flight attendant. Both vanish in an instant, and after several moments, his stomach still complaining, silencing his better sense, he resolves to follow the flight attendant's cart and beg for more. She sees him coming and, even before he asks, wordlessly hands him two more tiny packets, and he hurries back to his seat to force the cheese on the crackers and to gnaw at his remaining ice cubes. It is, he realizes, his first meal in more than a day. Two hours later a different flight attendant deposits a tray of chicken and rice before him and gives him a warning look. He forces himself not to bolt the food but to eat with excruciating slowness, forces himself to ignore the businessman's untouched tray, the man so intrigued by a silly movie he can't bring himself to eat, even after the flight attendant comes and takes away his own empty tray. When his fellow passenger abruptly rises to go to the toilet, the full tray gravitates to the empty spot in front of him, and without a pause, without even waiting for the man to reach the back of the plane, he bends his head low and shovels the cold meal into his mouth, then quickly slides the empty tray under his seat.

He reads about Mr. Lincoln. He sleeps. He stares. He navigates the aisle to the washroom, where the plane lurches and he pisses on his new shoes. *This is travel*, he tells himself. *I am traveling.*

Dawn breaks outside the oval windows and blinds them all. They are flying through the break of day, the actual point that separates the unstoppable day from cleaving night. He wants to wake the man beside him and crow, but he remembers Frances's words and hangs his head, biting back his excitement. Instead, he begins to catalog the now-visible clouds. Below them lies a heavy band of stratocumulus, like a line on a map separating one country from another. *The country below us may be under siege*, he thinks, *but we will fly on unhindered. It has nothing to do with us.* The captain's voice comes on the intercom to predict turbulence, but it's clear to one passenger at least that the weather up here is perfect, a clear blue bath with nary a single wave. Only when they begin the descent into a puffy bank of cumulus does he acknowledge the change coming.

It is not so easy in the next and final city. His entry there is like what he imagines it might be in the city of the dead. Weary, gray-faced, the passengers are divided by the color of their passports as

< 184 >

if those tidy books, like bank passbooks, reflect their worth. He is reminded anew that his country is not a good customer—it is, in fact, both pauper and spendthrift—and his passport, though new and bright, seems shabby and neglected. For the first time, as he glances at the other passports—blue, green, red—popping out all around him in the other lines, he also sees that his looks handmade. The seams are already loose. He hopes the pages don't fall out before he reaches the front of the line. A white man with the blank face of an ox on his way to market paws through his small suitcase, pausing briefly at Mr. Lincoln's story, while a thin-lipped woman scrutinizes his papers and questions his purpose for entering the country. He gives her the answer he practiced with Frances Okonjo, and she nods. "Student," he declares and is pleased at his truthfulness. Like Mr. Lincoln, he will never stop being a student. He too, he has vowed to himself, will master Euclidian dialogue—whatever that is. Nonetheless, he expects suspicion. He anticipates scorn, even minor violence, a roughed-up warning of a welcome. London knows better than to make entry easy for his kind; he knows and accepts, even honors, this. So the speed with which his papers and suitcase are returned and he is perfunctorily welcomed into the country astonishes him so much he nearly drops the lot and, against all Frances's good advice, stands gawking until the woman waves him away and he realizes that the light above the customs and immigration station has changed to green and the next in line, a horribly fatigued woman with an overburdened luggage cart, is scowling at him. Although no one halts him—he meanders through the airport uneasily—he feels as if he's under constant observation. It's quite possible, he hears Frances say in his head.

He left home with two crucial bits of information, both of which he was forbidden to commit to paper. The first: a map. Frances drew it out and made him copy it five times with her, then several times on his own—intricately colored diagrams that made the streets so visible

< 185 >

he could feel the pavement stones chafe beneath his thin shoes, the cold foreign air like a cap over his scalp.

Frances nodded approvingly. "You've a talent there as well, I see," she said, then she ripped up his beautiful copies and told him he was to draw the map again and again, at least a dozen times a day, until the day of his departure, when he was to burn all copies. After that he was to rely only on his memory. No one trusts a man bearing maps, for he is clearly a stranger.

Likewise, the number he was given after Frances left was to become a song in his head, a numeric melody of splits, splices, rounded wholes. He hummed it continuously so that its beat soon matched the internal rhythm of his own heart. Yes, he was wonderful with maps and numbers; none of this would prove problematic. He was such a good choice all around.

---

As a small child he had been tormented by nightmares—he can recall them still in Technicolor accuracy. His hands and legs as heavy as lead, he had been transformed into a pawn, a mere object, continually subjected to tortures by beings so evil and innovative, he could not even bear to recall their bestial faces. His parents lost patience with him; his father, worn to threads from lack of sleep, beat him out of frustration. He disturbed the entire neighborhood with his cries, which—an added insult—were girlishly high-pitched. Finally, an elderly aunt had taken him in for a few weeks to teach him how to navigate his dreams.

"You must come awake within them," she instructed him.

"I do!" he cried, and he nearly wept with anticipation of the next night, the sudden jar and strangled screams, his body soaked with sweat, writhing as his terrified eyes opened in the darkness and the nightmare swelled around him.

< 186 >

"No, little one," his aunt had said, "this is a different kind of wakefulness. You do not wake in *this world, but in that one.*" The problem, she told him, was that he was under a spell in his nightmare world and so lost all his powers. He must carry his strength from one world into the next. So, each night before bed, she helped him recite words to recall this boy, the one of many talents. It was a kind of incantation: *I am here. I am me. I am awake and can change this world.* Before long he learned to snap into focus even as he was under assault. He learned to laugh and command, to reorder his monsters. In his dreams he supervised a new construct—his devils became his crew—he remapped terror, squelching dark corners, plumping out shadows. With him in charge, no one rushed, certainly not at him. Soon his dreamtime world, so peaceful and controlled, became so boring that he abandoned it and slept in a deeper place, as if in an underground bunker, far away from the ting-ting industry of his hardworking demons.

Still, he remembered—both the torment and the solution. He knew what he must do to enter an alien land, to make it his own. The dreams had given him that. So many these days dismissed those nighttime wanderings, but he could attest to their power. Even Mr. Lincoln—so he'd read on the plane—had foreseen his own death in his dreams.

*Who has died?* Mr. Lincoln asked as he wandered through his sorrowed netherland a full ten days before John Wilkes Booth proclaimed victory.

*Why, the President,* came the grief-borne answer.

The bus driver does not glance at him as he boards, and he bumps his way to the middle of the bus, where a group of young men—a few with skin as dark as his own—dressed in nylon shorts and football jerseys occupy most of the seats. He sits gingerly beside one and receives a cheery smile as if they are mates, as if the fellow has been waiting for

< 187 >

him. This, in fact, is where he feels most comfortable, in the middle of a crowd of quietly boisterous men. He does not care much for female company. Before he'd agreed to this trip, when Frances thought he might refuse, she'd offered him a personal perk. Experimentally, he'd held her naked breasts, but he soon released them, shaking his head. She thinks him a gentleman; he is not.

It would have been difficult, no, impossible, for him to get the proper papers legally. He had a record, of course. In what was to have been his third year of university, he'd been arrested for setting a government building on fire. A derelict shack, once used as a post office (before that, yes, a police station), it had long since been abandoned. No one even slept there anymore; the wooden floors had fallen away. A dog had died trying to scramble out of the ruins, and the stench of its rank corpse eventually reached every one's cooking fire. They tasted the creature's death with every spoonful of food. If he had been a neighborhood hero, he would have simply poured gasoline, lit a match. Until now, however, no one has ever accused him of heroism. Then, he had borrowed a torch from Little Mo's body shop. He'd been teaching himself arc welding to impress a friend, a boy he loved at the university.

Oblivious to the pressing heat, the dry wood, the putrid odor—ignorant too of the rays of sparks each weld produced—he'd swung the torch too high, too wide. The fire was a growing rumble behind him as he examined the crooked wings of his welds. Pleased with the result, he'd waited around too long; white scars decorated his right leg and hip. He had other scars on his back from the beatings the guards had given him. His sentence was commuted only after a large bribe had been paid by an uncle. The same uncle also promised to compensate Uncle Mo for his loss and then put Frances onto him. Believing she had a real job to offer, his uncle had listed every possible attribute of his wayward nephew, most of them pure fabrications and none measuring the new sweep of his resentment. Frances could tell such claims were unlikely, but in the end, a simple test had determined his eminent suitability, and his ambition, that latent dog, allowed him to accept her generous offer.

---

When he arrives at the city hospital, he bypasses the main entrance and travels directly to the south entrance and the oncology wing. He does not pause at reception. Following Frances's map in his head, he finds the elevator banks and rides straight to the sixth floor. Only a few steps away from the door of Room 616 does he pause.

Inside Room 616 he finds the boy, who is only five years of age, the son of his third cousin Edward (who is also Frances's husband's brother) and a famous runway model named Otarine. The child's improbable name is Rupert, and asleep, he resembles an exquisite tea-colored cat: sleek, long-lashed, and perfect. Too perfect to be human, too perfect, truthfully, to exist. In fact, for the rest of his brief life, when he hears the word *beauty*, he will see the boy Rupert curled beneath his silken coverlet.

On a tray near the boy's bed is another meal: an untouched cutlet, a pile of whipped white potatoes with beautifully smooth brown gravy, brilliant green peas and diced jewel-like carrots. He has seen food like this only in movies. Another plastic dish is half filled with yellow Jell-O. Has he always been so hungry? He eats it all, his chest burning at the speed, and is slightly miffed that Rupert—or someone else—has consumed the other half of the Jell-O, which is tart and overly sweet at the same time and, he notices when he uses the adjoining washroom, has turned his tongue a brilliant gold.

Rupert sleeps on. No one interrupts them. Although it is midafternoon, the light in the hospital room is thin and wan, as if it too has a wasting disease. He is, he realizes, exhausted, and there is so much room left in the bed. Hectares of room. The bed is an entire countryside, with plenty of space for a visitor. As he crawls between the sheets, he thinks, for the first time since he agreed to Frances's proposal, of the connection between himself and this boy. They *are* countrymen. They share blood.

For the first time in years, Patrick dreams. He is still traveling, but this is not the familiar, riotous landscape of his childhood nightmares. He's landed in a quieter, denser place that he finds equally frightening. He feels himself flailing, his bare soles sinking into gray ash in these colorless, empty streets, but then, all at once, as if his aunt has been whispering in his ear, he remembers. And then he spies the boy, perched wearily on a gray curb.

"Halloo, Rupert," he says, offering the boy his hand.

The boy ignores him. His eyes are riveted on a distant thunderhead, a burring wind. Approaching? Departing? It's hard to say.

"A perfect match!" the doctor had declared, and yet lying here beside the boy, he feels the weighted air. He smells the rain, the storm passing or descending. Awake in his dream, he senses the child sinking in front of him. It's a slow, aching fall, and nothing will stop it. If the rain comes, the dust will disappear and the boy as well. He considers the child's hand, resting in his own. "A perfect match!" a doctor pronounced, and Frances's phone jumped into her hand. "Edward!" she had shrieked, as if calling to the other side of the moon, "Edward!" Frances's voice resounds in his ears, an ongoing trumpet that only rouses him when he opens his eyes and sees a beautiful woman bending close to him:

"Edward! Edward!" she is crying—right here in Room 616.

His cousin recognizes him at once, although they were just lanky boys not much older than Rupert last time they met. In his great success as a politician, Edward has become both shorter and more muscular. With his stern brown features, he gives the impression

< 190 >

that he is made of something dense and impervious, a precious metal, perhaps. He wears a gorgeous blue shirt, of a shade that matches the unadulterated sky beyond the clouds. His wife towers over him. She is a slice of a woman. He can hardly comprehend her looks, which are both frightening and exquisite. She is all lips and liquid eyes and legs like stripped-down stalks. Flashes of Rupert's lovely skin. And yet he can't fully see her. He is squinting, blinking rapidly, aching to get her into focus. It's odd, he thinks, that it is often easier to see within one's dreams than while awake.

"Otarine," Edward says, "this is my cousin, Patrick Egbagbe. He has arrived."

The boy, who awakened with his mother's cries, is mewling now for her attention, and she falls to her knees beside the bed. She stretches one arm over her son, embracing him, and—at the same time—she reaches out to take Patrick's hand. She is weeping, he sees, and for a long moment, he cannot move, can only grasp that delicate cool hand in an awkward arc over the child and nod. Rupert's dull eyes shift to Patrick.

"Halloo, then," he says, surprising everyone.

The hospital is not quite ready for Patrick. The results from the tests Frances had set up for him had been sent ahead, but for the moment his blood is drawn into test tubes, which are capped and labeled and trundled away.

"Why are they starting again?" Otarine asks. They had left her in the boy's room, but now she's beside Edward and Patrick in the lab, a knife edge between them.

"They must be certain," Edward tells her. It would be worse for Rupert, he assures her, if an incompatibility exists.

"After all this," she says. "All these preparations. And if it doesn't work." She eyes Patrick.

"We'll start again." At this, Edward offers a barely perceptible nod in Patrick's direction, as if to warn his wife that they are not alone.

"You must be exhausted," Edward says to Patrick, while Otarine sinks into a chair.

He wonders when they slept last themselves.

"I'll stay, darling," Edward tells her. "Take my cousin home."

She argues; he presses her.

"The baby," Edward says.

"Exactly," Otarine counters. "How can you expect me to—"

"Otarine," Edward insists. "You must." His cousin squeezes Patrick's shoulder as they leave. *Good of you*, he hears. *We'll take care*...And that's it.

There is a car with a driver waiting, but despite his stolen nap, Patrick can barely inch his eyes open, and the man remains a shadow. Otarine does not introduce them. Patrick follows his cousin's wife into the preposterously generous backseat, where she collapses into a corner, and together they are transported wordlessly through London's blank wet streets, streets that remind Patrick of Otarine's tear-stained face. *The entire city is mourning with them*, he thinks, as his own burning eyes drift closed. It reminds him of the book he'd read on the airplane—the days right after Mr. Lincoln's death, a city draped in black bunting.

———

Rupert, it turns out, is not his cousin's only child. When, hours later, Patrick wakes in his room at Edward and Otarine's, a girl of about eight is standing beside his bed in a rosebud nightgown. She too is tea-colored and lovely, with Otarine's wide almond eyes.

"It's the baby," she informs Patrick by way of greeting. "She won't stop."

And Patrick hears it then, a horrendous wailing, that distressing siren that sets his own heart to keening. He leaps from the bed, surprised to find himself wearing pajamas, silk and cotton with a lavender stripe. They are the most beautiful garments he has ever seen, even more than his cousin's shirt. He would like to admire them more, but the girl is leading him out into the hallway, where the siren wails are even louder. It's the sound, he realizes, he's been waiting to hear since he began his journey: anguish, despair, fury all riveted together, a burning ash that he's heading toward.

In a dimly lit room at the end of the hallway, Otarine paces while a red-faced infant struggles against her shoulder. The baby rocks violently back and forth, slamming her tiny face into the woman's narrow shoulder again and again, howling with indignation at each self-inflicted blow. One side of Otarine's silk dressing gown is soaked, darkened by the baby's tears and spit, the sweat that soaks her tiny head. An elderly woman bustles into the room. She offers a bottle of warmed milk, which the baby rejects with renewed wailing.

"She won't, ma'am," the woman tells Otarine.

"She must, she must."

The bottle is jammed back at the baby, who evades it, shaking her head violently. His cousin's wife's voice is all new to Patrick. Deeper, harsher, nothing like the gentle woman at the hospital. The burnished skin has grayed, and the sleek line of her head is marred by her unkempt hair, which springs in all directions. When she catches sight of the girl and Patrick, both jump a little at the burnt snap of her gaze.

"*Albertine!*" this new Otarine bellows. "*Go back to bed.*"

The girl shifts a little in an illusion of flight, but she doesn't actually move. It's a neat trick Patrick admires: motion that is not motion. Yet it doesn't fool the girl's mother.

"*Go...back...to...bed,*" she bawls again over the baby's wails. Instead, as if summoned, Patrick enters the room and peels the baby from a shocked Otarine—who does not protest. You can see what a weight the infant has become by the way the woman sinks at her release. Patrick has barely settled the baby against his chest when the siren cries ease into hiccups, as if the infant is descending from a great altitude; a knob has been flicked, and then there is silence. He completes one full circuit around the bedroom, a formality, before he lays the baby into its crib and retreats to Albertine's side again.

"How— " Otarine begins. She dares to lay a hand on the infant's belly, stunned by the child's regular breathing.

"She's asleep," she marvels.

"It's just something that happens," Patrick tries to tell her. "My mother used to say I smell like sweet grass in the wind. Babies pause to listen to the phantom shushing, and the scent eases them. Certain lions give off the same odor, she told me; it's why their prey acquiesce so easily."

Albertine takes the opportunity to sniff Patrick.

"Cake, Mother," she tells Otarine. "Lemon pound cake."

"Albertine," her mother warns.

Meanwhile, the elderly woman—Otarine calls her Cora, as in *now, Cora, now*—sprints into action, adjusting a baby monitor, dowsing the lamp on a nightstand. The sudden darkness, so promising in its silence, propels the group into the hallway, and the woman gently shuts the door, grasps Albertine's hand, and whisks her down the hall.

"Goodnight, Mother," the girl whispers back at them loudly. "Mother, Mother, goodnight."

"I must bathe," Patrick declares in the hallway. "It's been days."

Otarine, gazing at the closed door, clutches her neck.

"I always smell the same," Patrick reassures her.

She nods and drifts down the hallway, one hand pressed against her forehead. Half asleep, she has to remember how to walk, it seems, her long legs placed so carefully like those of a crane. She pauses once to look back, and again Patrick glimpses the fragmented beauty from the hospital. She murmurs across her shoulder, but before Patrick can manage his own goodnight wishes, she vanishes into another room and shuts the door behind her, leaving him alone in the dark.

Albertine is waiting when Patrick emerges from his bath. She wears the cowed expression of a half-starved dog who knows he will be beaten but must rush in and nuzzle around for scraps nonetheless. The clock reads twenty minutes to four, and it's pitch-black outside the tall multipaned window, but Albertine is fully dressed in what must be her school uniform: a pleated red plaid skirt, white blouse, navy jumper. Her hair has been braided inexpertly.

"You are ready to go," he says.

"In case," she tells Patrick, "Mother will take me with her today."

"Today is still hours away," he says.

"I'll rest here," Albertine says. "That way I won't get too comfortable." And she lies down on his bed and dutifully shuts her eyes.

In the bathroom Patrick had debated whether or not he should dress in his own clothes, sour from the journey, or continue to wander about in these fine pajamas. Now he's glad to be fully dressed, ready to go into the day. The hallway is quiet, and he can't recall where the stairs are, so it takes some time to navigate his way. A faint clatter leads him to the kitchen, which is down many winding steps. Albertine's talk of lemon cake has made him hungry once more. Through the open door he spies the same elderly woman, Cora, who brought the baby her bottle, now setting out bowls, pulling down a heavy-looking fry pan from a copper rack.

"Mr. Patrick, is it? Our miracle worker," the woman says when she spots him. "Come in here now. You must be starved."

The brightness of the kitchen revives him, and in seconds Cora has real food before him, a warmed plate of soft buttery eggs, white toast, and bacon.

"I've got the coffee going," she tells him. "Mr. Edward likes it too, you see."

He forces himself to eat slowly, reassured by her care. More toast appears, more bacon. Another spoonful of eggs is ladled onto his plate. Finally he pushes himself away from the table. Cora is straining to reach a bin of flour set on a high shelf. Patrick easily brings it down for her, places it beside a marble counter. His pulse quickens a little. Here is something he can do. With his stomach full, he can think again. A number dances in his head, that now-familiar tune waiting to be hummed aloud, but there is time yet.

Another cup is placed on the table.

"Please sit," he tells Cora, ushering her to a stool along the long counter. "I have questions. That baby."

"Oh," she says. But the coffee is poured, and Patrick is waiting. "Just for a moment."

"They'd hoped, you see, the baby would have been a match. They could have used the, oh, dear, what's it called? The cord blood, that's it. But little Rupert is a special case. Unusual. One in a million. We thought his mother would die when they found out the new baby's blood disappointed." Cora shakes her head. "You could not imagine such grief, young man." She pauses, sips her coffee. "But then you came along, didn't you?" she says.

While she talks, Patrick mixes a dough, adding a tiny splash of vinegar. He cuts in cold butter, folds and lifts, gathers and shapes. He finds blackberry preserves and apricot jam in a cupboard and has the dough rolled out, cut, and filled before Cora emerges from her reverie.

"Well, son," she says. "You are indeed a man of many skills."

He pours her another cup of coffee.

"Go on," he says, waving a pastry brush. "Now, Albertine."

At five-thirty, just as Patrick is pulling a tray from the oven, his cousin Edward appears in the kitchen, once again dressed in his beautiful clothes. Patrick has to restrain himself from stroking the fine weave of his cousin's elegant suit coat.

"Cora," Edward says, eyeing the pastries, "you will save all our lives."

Was it Patrick's imagination, or did a picture of an ashen Rupert just appear on the kitchen wall above the wall ovens? Everyone's eyes skitter to avoid the boy's unblinking stare, and Edward's shoulders slump. He shakes his head again and again, wipes his eyes.

"She loves those, you know. I had forgotten."

They don't hear her approaching. Cora is scrubbing baking pans under a loud sluice of water in the porcelain sink, and Edward is explaining to Patrick how that day they will begin giving him something called Filgrastim, which will increase his blood count.

"You may feel a little sick, the doctor said, but just a bit. Like a light flu, aches and pains, maybe a headache. Nothing a strong young man can't endure."

Patrick tries to imagine what this will be like, but all he can envision is a surging within him, a powerful elevation that will sweep him off his feet.

A reassembled Otarine, newly glossy and self-possessed, enters the kitchen, bearing the infant whose name, Patrick has learned, is Evangeline. The child is squabbling with the world again, staccato half cries that catch painfully in her throat, but Otarine knows just what to do. She deposits the baby, not in the infant seat attached to the high chair, but—to Edward's surprise—in Patrick's lap.

"Otarine," Edward protests, but she merely raises her forefinger.

A lull descends on the kitchen as the baby composes herself and with great presence begins to survey her surroundings. She is, they all realize, clearly her mother's daughter: regal, aloof, desirable. Each one of the adults falls in love a little with her at that moment, even Patrick, who is fascinated by how well this baby can contain the fury she carries like a bumptious seed within her. At his request Cora brings Patrick a yellow bowl and a tiny spoon. He begins to feed the

< 197 >

child, and before their eyes she transforms back into a pretty infant, greedily smacking her lips over each spoonful of applesauce. In between bites she considers them all, curious at last and, oddly, even more controlling.

*Yes*, he silently reassures the child, *this is exactly how you come awake.*

Otarine goes wild over the pastries, Patrick's own version of a fruit Viennoiserie, filled with lemon custard and blackberry, glazed with apricot jam. She gulps madly at the air as if the aroma alone might satisfy her, even as Edward tears away a tiny flaky piece and slips it into her lovely mouth. Otarine groans with pleasure; Cora begins to explain; Patrick shakes his head. In the midst of all the feeding—Patrick with Evangeline; Edward with Otarine—a rumpled Albertine slips into the chair beside her mother.

"Oh, darling," Otarine coos, "you must taste this! This is...sustenance. This is...*food of the gods.*"

She makes munching noises beside the girl and actually reaches out to smooth the child's hair. Patrick can feel Albertine vibrating from across the room and knows too that it won't be long until the girl's great need will wear away Otarine's goodwill once more.

But *shush*, he tells himself. That storm, like so many others, like the inevitable undoing, may be sidestepped for the moment now that he's finally here in this, his new country, now that he's safe on the ground, undetectable.

# MADHOUSE

My cousin Eldie lives in a 4,000-square-foot house that took twelve years to build. A mad framer called the shots, redrawing the plans at will and tucking treasures—river rocks, top-end screws, his ex-wife's jewelry—in the rafters to be found...by whom? Why, the equally mad electrician, of course, who arrived too late, too late, and ripped apart the vapor barrier and the stiff needled clouds of pink insulation. This electrician believed the others who had come *before* him, who did not know him, who did not even know he'd be hired for the job, had conspired against him, making his job "a living hell." He bound himself in wires and nearly set the place in flames, right-wing rants blaring from his car radio. A mad plumber ran pipes in and out of walls and tuned them so the house would sing dirges as water heated and the tub filled. Closets vanished off the plans, electrical outlets appeared on ceilings, a thin line of mold appeared beneath the torn vapor barrier before the mad sheet-rocker arrived and sealed the ruin tight. The tile guy, highly recommended, scrapped Eldie's subtle design and claimed artistic license, floor to ceiling, so that two steps into the bathrooms, a visitor, dizzied and disoriented, might end up mistaking a tiled dip in the wall for a quirky urinal. Finish carpenters went crazy in that house, held their breath, installed cabinets with manic speed, then fled. Insanity all round, and I haven't even talked about the well-digger with the voodoo stick, the roofer with the reefer, the trio—frightened by a moose—who refused to step out of their truck and instead delivered two woodstoves up the neighbor's rutted gravel road, leaving them beside the woodpile with a caustic note.

< 199 >

(Did I mention this was in Alaska?)

But the house, eventually, was finished. And Eldie, her husband, and the three kids moved in. Were they mad before? It's hard to remember, but once they took up residence, the entire family began scouring the recycling bin to collect drinking containers—empty salsa tubs and yogurt cartons and filmy jam jars—and ate off the battered dishes they shared with two dogs. Unpacking that wedding china, even the pots and pans they'd used in their old cabin, seemed too much of a task. Boxes of carelessly sealed possessions were carried off to a storage unit they'd visit perhaps once a year. Over time they covered the walls with outdated maps and the fine wood floors with twelve lost seasons of discarded shoes. Now, on Friday nights, like any normal family, they eat takeout pizza and watch movies, the five of them swinging from hammocks strung across the crooked corners of what was meant to be a great room but, altered by a mad contractor, instead resembles the deck of a famous ship that failed to reach its destination and instead was forever becalmed, ghosting on an orphaned sea.

< 200 >

# CATCH, RELEASE

Two split-tailed ravens strut across the roof. Another lands, the one they've been waiting for, the one with the rock, the flattened tennis ball, the boon of a silver Christmas tree ornament tossed inadvertently in the rubbish. The raven flies to the peak of the roof, considers angles, distances between peak and edge, his compatriots' studied indifference. He waits even as one of the others pecks at the roof as if he's determined to chip out his own toy from the asphalt shingles. Only when a crescendo of complaint begins does the raven release and let roll, transforming the chorus into joyous cackles and a maddened rush to retrieve.

You think this is funny? You think this is play?

It's all about loss. Don't kid yourself. Even a simple game of catch is hinged on the moment the ball leaves the glove, the moment it returns. Don't even try to think this story or any other story is about something else.

They were in the church, and Eddie's memorial service had just ended. Without a coffin, without a body, the gathering had felt incomplete. So, when Digger Fowler, the old funeral director, clutched at the sleeve of Nora's best navy-blue jacket and drew her to an alcove beside the baptismal fount, she followed expectantly. The old man's slurred speech was incomprehensible at first, and Nora, conscious of the others waiting to offer their condolences, tried to edge away. But Digger Fowler caught her with his ramblings, words that seemed to enter her ear in disarray, sorting themselves into sense even as his mouth stopped moving and he pulled away to regard her reaction.

"Who can be sure?" he whispered to her. "No records, beyond recognition. Did I see his face? No, I did not. I would swear it...stack of bibles. I did not.

"Oh, he'd never leave you, darling," Digger Fowler insisted, his fingers pressing into Nora's arm. "Rest assured. He's waiting for the moment."

*What moment?* thirteen-year-old Rose wondered. She leaned heavily on the pillar between her mother and the undertaker, waiting for Digger Fowler to speak again. Too tender-hearted for his job, he spoke out of kindness, unwilling to merely shake her mother's hand and express his sorrow that Rose's dad was dead. But her mother was no fool, was she?

"The island," Nora said, softly. "Of course."

In the undertaker's theory, her father never died. The night of the accident, the Aid Squad had cut a poor, burnt body from a car (Nora's car, in fact) and taken it to St. Michael's Hospital, where they took one look and sent it on to Fowler's Funeral Home. Yet the next morning, the body—still presumed to be Eddie—was gone. Old Fowler's son apologized like crazy to Nora. Apparently, the body, confused with another, had been sent on for cremation. But Digger Fowler wondered, one eyebrow raised, *Was the body Eddie's?* After all, in a most telling coincidence, Eddie's small sailboat, *Windspinner*, had lost its mooring that night, only to be found swamped a mile or so down the Mill beach, aimed in the direction of the island where Eddie grew up, the island he missed and talked about at every opportunity.

No one lived on Eddie's island anymore. Just the scavenging gulls and raccoons, the black-tailed deer, and slant-eyed wild goats. Those gossiping ravens. The wells had all dried up, and State Wildlife had bought the few miles of craggy rock and forest meadow. Only a couple

< 202 >

of ancient sisters and a retired farmer had remained at that point, all too creaky to do more than tend their vegetable patches, until they agreed to leave their gray frame houses and tumbledown barns, take the state money, and move on. Eddie had been okay until then, until he read about the closed mail ferry and witnessed the last shuttle of islander goods arriving in Salish Bay.

"Oh, he took that badly, didn't he, dear?" Digger Fowler had whispered to Nora. "I'd say for certain, he was not in his right mind."

Nora had never been to the island. Even the motion of the town ferry, toddling back and forth across the placid bay from peninsula to peninsula, was too much for Rose's mother. A single excursion could make her violently ill. A trip to the island, farther away, across rougher water, was out of the question. If only she could *see* him there, she told Rose, if she could know the island the way he did, she could hold on until he was ready to come home. But how? Who could paint for her the portrait of Eddie, happy again, slowly gaining his strength so that he could come back to her? Eddie had been the baby of the island. Only a few old folks, missing persons themselves with their memories in pieces, carried the island still.

---

After days of searching, Nora lit on the Mary Flower Home: a sprawling one-story, heavily ramped structure behind a nearly dead privet hedge. She charmed her way into the nursing home, explaining her purpose in a way that made her sound sane, as if she were a local historian enamored with the abandoned island. Rose was left to follow, slinking in her mother's shadow, averting her eyes from the shrunken occupants of wheelchairs, wraiths who faced the walls and plaintively crooned, or worse, were so drugged that Rose imagined they were already dead and simply propped up around the place to convey an aura of gruesome prosperity. Only twenty souls resided at

Mary Flower and, compared with other nursing home patients, their lucidity was striking. Here, the residents were not only forthcoming, they were more inclined to bypass their adult lives and skip back to their own childhood days where Nora lurked, yearning for a mention of the island where her husband had grown up, and where—she was nearly positive now—he might be waiting.

Rose came along because she did not like the new emptiness of the house or the possibility that their neighbor, Mrs. Falcon, herself not long bereaved, would arrive on the doorstep. Old Mrs. Falcon had discovered (as a result of a recent past life reading) that she had once been a renowned baker, destined to do good with her pastry. She persisted in providing Rose and her mother with plate after plate of hard, iced buns or lopsided petit fours, dry as dust on the tongue. She even shared with them a cake shaped—Mrs. Falcon proudly announced—like the face of her grandson, a troubled boy she barely knew, a boy she had agreed to take in upon his release from Juvie in two weeks. As a cake, the grandson, with his long, ugly face and hooded marzipan eyes, was not promising. He looked like Abe Lincoln gone pirate. Rose hoped for better things from the actual boy. She tried to imagine him as Tom Ungar, a tenant of her grandfather. Once, in the kitchen of her grandfather's house, Tom Ungar had lifted his long blond ponytail and invited Rose to stroke a tiny ebony angel tattooed on the back of his neck.

Mrs. Falcon told Rose and Nora that her grandson was in Juvie because he missed too much school. Later, she amended his crime, telling Rose's mother that "kids that age are so impressionable. They have no sense of time. They want everything now."

Then: "People shouldn't leave expensive things out where children can find them."

"He's a thief, Rose," her mother told her when they were alone. "We better lock up your dad's tools."

< 204 >

# Catch, Release

They still had the house, one of a pair built by two unmarried brothers as an isolated homestead. Now, the twin frame farmhouses—theirs and Mrs. Falcon's—were simply the last in a long line of houses out on River Run Road. They had the truck, of course. The rent on Rose's father's boat shop was paid up nearly six months in advance due to a scraping and caulking job (his first in months) he had done for the port landlord. The garden was mulched, garlic sprouting in the far corner, raspberry canes pruned and ready for staking. They had stacks and stacks of dry firewood: madrona and quick-burning fir. The pantry was full of tinned fish—sockeye and halibut caught by Rose's father—and blackberry conserve from a family effort last August. Clothes in closets; boots in the hall; a box of tools in the corner of the mudroom. Saturday afternoons the radio persisted in playing the blues show he loved until his heart had grown so sore he would slam out of the house with a desperate glance. Gone, but not. Missing, yet found daily: here and here and here. Both of them jumping at the sounds of the cat creaking the upstairs floorboards, the visiting ravens cavorting on the roof. Both of them waiting.

Somehow they made it to March, late afternoon, a Sunday. All morning long, at the Mary Flower, Nora interrogated wizened crones and incontinent old men who sat with their bathrobes open, flys undone on their yellowed boxer shorts, while Rose perched on a chair in the television lounge among wheelchairs, perhaps the only one actually watching *The Little Mermaid*. A social director had made a move to take Rose under her wing, plying the girl with half-sized plastic cups of fruit juice or Jell-O that left a metallic aftertaste. The morning wore them both out, and when the afternoon visitors began to arrive, Nora took Rose home. It was only two o'clock in the afternoon, but Rose was half-asleep when the rickety truck left the pavement and bounced into the gravel drive. She opened her eyes in time to witness a tiny figure dressed in an orange terrycloth sweat-suit leap before them, causing Nora to swerve the truck desperately.

"What in god's name…?" Nora began, stalling the engine. "Oh," she said, her voice already let down, "it's Claudine."

"I just wanted to tell you," the old lady said, leaning in through Nora's window, "that Gordon's arrived."

It took a few minutes for Rose and her mother to recall Claudine Falcon's delinquent grandson.

"He's had some troubles. He's just skin and bones," Claudine confided as she had several weeks ago when she first agreed to take in the boy. Her face was rosy from the wind.

Rose thought she looked a little hysterical. As always, Rose wondered if Mrs. Falcon was all right in the head. Here she was, beaming as if her grandson's juvenile record was an achievement.

"And what a tired boy! He's been sleeping since they dropped him off."

Rose cringed and glanced toward the upstairs windows of the Falcons' house, half-expecting to see the curtains shift. Wedged under the peeling madronas beside the barn was a beat-up silver car that Rose supposed the grandson had brought with him.

"Rose," Claudine said, "you'll come over later and meet Gordon, huh? I've been baking."

Rose concentrated on her shoes, the same too-tight black flats she'd worn to her father's memorial service, and waited for her mother to refuse the invitation for her.

"Give a call when the boy wakes up," Nora said instead, restarting the truck to park it beside the old barn. "I'll send her over."

"Mom," Rose began when they were alone.

"Later, Rose," Nora said. "Please."

# Catch, Release

―――――――――

Once the bathroom door closed, the faucet roar deafening her mother to the threatened phone call, Rose changed into jeans and a sweatshirt. She slipped on her boots and took the path to the river. Dark, spongy, nearly overgrown, this trail and the plants that lined it belonged to her father. All of it. He'd taught her the names: the lady's tresses, the sprawling purslane, the clumps of fireweed, the delicate umbrellas of enchanter's nightshade—each distinct shape clustering into green anonymity. She could almost feel him rustling under the shadows like the all-seeing animals that used the river as a drinking hole. Deer sometimes crashed through the snowberries, one ungainly leg after another, while on the opposite bank, a narrow trail served as a byway for lean, half-wild dogs, so intent upon their journeys that they seldom did more than glance at Rose, never breaking a trot.

The late afternoon sun crawled over the rock where Rose sat. Last winter, she and her father had been right here when he spotted a cougar above them, perched in a tree asleep. Thin and rangy, a mottled beast, it looked nothing like the sleek animal that was part of her plastic toy collection. Rose found it hard to believe the cougar was real. Following her father's instructions, she backed up the trail toward home, raising her hands above her head to make herself tall the way she'd been taught. She rushed into old Ule Falcon and babbled out the story of the cougar, pointing down the trail to where she'd left her father. Ule went looking for the cougar with a gun. Thought he'd shot it but found only the slightest trail of blood.

"Poor starving thing," her father said to her mother when he came in a half-hour later. "Even from that distance, I could count its bones." Eddie's eyes were bright for the first time in days, an old coiled energy apparent in the way he leaned against the kitchen counter. He had kept the animal in his sight until Ule and his gun appeared out of nowhere. Her father nearly wrestled the old man down.

Nora had feigned concern, but she too had momentarily changed, lost the hovering, worried expression. Rose danced around the kitchen, raising her arms and catching her parents' hands in an eager demonstration that made them all laugh. They made a feast of nachos and guacamole and watched a comedy that made them giddy, but later Rose woke in the middle of the night to her father's pacing. She heard the doors creaking, the far-off rumble of his restlessness.

For months, Rose wished the cougar back. She carried scraps from the kitchen to place in the crook of the tree, sure that it was the cougar that carried the half-eaten sandwiches away, even after she interrupted a pair of ravens lolling on the rock, yanking tongues of ham from between bread. Passersby, those ravens. Her father said they liked to cause trouble because they were too smart for the idle life they'd been handed. Their animal chores easily accomplished, only mischief guided them.

She liked to lie on the rock and daydream, mulling over the tricks of ravens and so clearly imagining the cougar chasing them away that she was not surprised that afternoon in March when she opened her eyes to spot, between flighty shadows, a figure in the tree. Seconds later, the boy's black eyes met hers, and Rose panicked. She fled up the trail, forgetting every caution her father had taught her about facing danger in the wild.

———————

In the morning there was no sight of the grandson at the bus stop or at Salish Bay Middle School, but in the late afternoon when Rose wandered back up the driveway, kicking gravel, she saw him. A tallish boy with a shock of black hair, perched on the hood of the old strange car. He was smoking furiously, a grocery bag tilted beside him. Mrs.

< 208 >

Falcon's own car, a gray Buick, was gone. Nora, too, was still at work, balancing accounts for Rose's grandfather's rentals.

Rose waved, hoping that would be enough, but the boy slid off the car and, grabbing the paper bag, approached her.

"Hey,' he said, crushing his cigarette under one black boot. He held the bag out to her. "From my grandmother."

Rose took a step backward into the weeds beside the driveway. "A cake?" she asked.

"Pie," Gordon said. "Who knows what kind."

Although he looked fierce and serious, Gordon's voice was gentle, almost girlish.

Rose felt a little sorry for him stuck out here with his grandmother, the reborn baker.

Gordon put the bag down. "Yours?" he asked, nodding toward the strange car.

"I thought it was yours."

"There's a note on the dashboard for someone named Nora."

Rose said, "Let me see."

The car was from her grandfather.

"You mean he's just giving it to you?" Gordon said.

Her grandfather rented the lower half of his old Victorian in town to a group of brothers who fancied themselves a motorcycle gang. They called themselves "The Phantom Corps." Her mother called them "the lost Ungar boys." The Phantoms never seemed to pay their rent in cash. Tools, car parts, welded sculptures, old tape decks, even a chicken house—such was the currency that passed between Rose's grandfather and his tenants. When the Maverick appeared, her grandfather thought of Nora and the old truck. He had Tom Ungar drive it right over to Little River Road, his solution to a problem Nora had not yet acknowledged.

"She won't want it," Rose told her new neighbor.

"What will you do with it?" he asked.

Rose shrugged.

"Let's get it outta there," Gordon said.

Deep violet stains splotched the red vinyl interior, and the car stank of cigarette smoke. A dozen or more slits riddled the cracked dashboard, each filled with a matchbook from places as diverse as the Sea Grift Motor Inn on the Oregon coast and Candy Jane's, a strip joint in a place Gordon immediately proclaimed he had to visit—Candy, Alaska. The seat had been ripped out of the back, leaving just the molded gray metal form of the car's underbody, with pieces of a brown, hairy undercarpet stacked on one side. Gordon and Rose sat in the Maverick for a half hour, reading the matchbooks and the surprisingly pristine owner's manual they found (along with a pair of bright yellow panties and one pink mitten, filthy in its palm) in the glove box. Tom Ungar had left the key in the ignition and when Gordon turned it, the Grateful Dead slammed into their heads.

Gordon was triumphant. He was glowing. He paced around the car, admiring it, so absorbed it took him a while to realize Rose was staring at him.

"What?" he said.

"You look like your cake," Rose blurted out.

Nora arrived home just as Rose was explaining how Mrs. Falcon had captured his square-jawed gawkiness in a three-layer *dacquoise* that had had the misfortune to have been made with rancid butter. Rose watched her mother drag her work folders and a grocery bag from the truck. She knew her mother wouldn't notice the car. They had to point it out to her. They made her come closer, examine the details.

"It looks like the car of a serial killer," she said.

Her eyes slipped back toward Eddie's steadfast green truck. Beside it, the Maverick looked like a flashy slut, sleeping off a bender in the woods. Rose worried that her mother would want the car removed, but by the time Nora wandered across the lawn and through the back door, she had forgotten Rose's new car.

The Maverick was nearly out of gas. Before dinner Gordon drained the gas tank of the seldom-used RV that had been the reason for Ule Falcon's specially built garage. Gordon knew something of engines, he said, but Rose had to show him where the dipstick was, where to pour the can of thirty-weight oil they found in the Falcons' garage. By ten o'clock, the women of both households were asleep, and Rose and Gordon met by the barn.

"I'll drive first," Gordon said, and he slipped behind the wheel.

---

For weeks, Nora was the soul of patience, the darling of the elderly, who, floating above the unfamiliar landscape of their current lives, needed to tug continually on the strings of memory, that gnarled wire that still secured them to the earth. Nora anchored their ancient hands, while they tested themselves, stroking that thread with a wavering volubility. She heard tales of childhood pleasures (new dresses, old dogs, feasts scratched from a single ingredient—meals more delicious than any that came in the more prosperous years that followed) and childhood pains (hair curled in paper with hot tongs, castor oil, woodshed beatings). The old people regaled her with stories of peculiar habits: the unemployed father who kept a notebook, recording each nuance of the passing day; the mother who would only eat alone in the kitchen; the sister who fell weekly from the barn loft after wrestling with an imaginary suitor.

And the clothes! She was deluged with wardrobes: beaded hats and tiny strapped shoes and gloves buttoned up the sides, spring suits of pale blue linen, crepe party dresses with hand-stitched lace collars, winter furs, foundation garments—garters and girdles and slip straps biting shoulders—muffs and fur caps. She heard the firsts: a dance,

< 211 >

a radio, a car, the first refrigerator replacing the icebox and the ice-
man with his ever-patient nag. The lasts: ancient mothers turned
into babbling children, recriminations at the bedside, the back door
closing quietly, the front door slamming, the car, alone, the silent
phone. Weather: the roof that blew off the police station, the icicles
on the milkman's handlebar mustache, the fine hot nights that had
children lined up under thin blankets on the summer lawn. The war,
old friends, the war, the Depression, the lost house, the lost hope, the
open hand. Secrets bottled up for decades were exhumed in incoher-
ent whispers that brought on weeping fits and pride so tender Nora,
who had to turn her face away as if she were presented with an open
wound, remained incapable of seeing a connection between their lives
and her own mission.

Patient—oh, she was so patient! Weeks went by before she heard of
an outing to the island, a simple beach picnic long before Eddie's time.

Imagine finding a scrap of fabric, a square inch of pale, lavender
linen with shredded edges and a hole in the weaving. Imagine sitting
night after night with this forsaken relic, weaving the threads back
into orderly lines that seem to lengthen and straighten with every
pass of a careful needle until finally the edges are looped and expertly
bound, and what is left is a miniature but wholly perfect garment.
This is what Nora did with a simple, half-fabricated memory from
a strange, wispy-haired woman named Winckett, who released that
long-ago picnic to Rose's mother. Nora snatched it up and re-worked
it as her own.

In the memory, there was a family picnic. On the island's beach,
Nora filled her pockets with smooth beach stones, the flat green ag-
ates that lined the western shore. Stones she could imagine Eddie
collecting on the rare warm day. She dragged a stick along the tideline
and pounced upon the clam holes, jumping back before the stream of

water shot out. She ate a piece of fried chicken and a tiny tart green apple and drank water from a canteen. Sand blew into the rice pudding, but she ate that, too, spooning in the grit with the smooth. Through everything, she kept looking over her shoulder for Eddie's approach, despite the fact that the picnic occurred some thirty years before his birth. She wandered, and when the picnic boat left, Nora was marooned on the darkening beach. The thin moon rose and the black beach transformed itself into a photograph of shadows. Whole families of raccoons waddled toward the water, their tidy hands rummaging in the stones for a forgotten half-crust, an apple core. She huddled into herself, closing her eyes against the unusually light wind that hummed around her ears. When she opened them, the raccoons were gone and Eddie, years younger than she had known him, crouched beside her. As if she were a stranger, he showed her how to plunge her cool hands into the hill of stones beneath her. She pressed her hands and bare feet deep down to where the hidden stones, like forgotten coals, still contained the day's heat. Her eyes closed in pleasure. She held her hands there until that warmth too dissolved and Eddie was gone.

Through this one memory, Nora composed the island beach. She tried for more: the trail through the scrim of trees to the fields, the narrow, overgrown path leading up the bluff house that Eddie's great-grandfather had built. She scoured local natural history books, but the photographs, wonderful in their individual context, could not be applied to the vague outlines of a dream. Nora felt her loss acutely. The landscape receded, the fabric stretched to its breaking point. She ate only soda crackers for a week, her heart half-broken again. Even Rose could not claim her attention. Nora let the girl fend for herself, hardly noticing how Gordon had taken up residence at their kitchen table, eating soup from tins with Rose, watching television as Rose watched her.

"Mom," Rose called again and again, her voice like a distant ring-ing telephone.

"Mom."

"In a minute," Nora whispered, closing her eyes.

In the trees outside, the ravens mimicked. First, they performed their imitation of the cats. The trees resounded with plaintive meows that caused every feline in the vicinity to slink low and take cover, but Nora paid the ravens no mind until one of them tried *his* voice, a single low note from a favorite blues song. Then she lingered in the drive, holding her breath so that even that slight interruption wouldn't mask the sound she desperately wanted to hear. The ravens pelted her with cedar berries, urging her to wake up, but she wouldn't budge, and disgusted, they flew away, imitating her weeping as they went: *Uhnuh-uhnuh waawaawaa.*

They didn't mean to be cruel. It was just a game to them.

Not for Nora. She tried for more at the Mary Flower Home, but the old woman who supplied that thinnest of images was as coy as the ravens. That Mrs. Winckett, an island widow. She teased Nora, claiming kinship to the island as well as a memory that emerged and receded as drastically as a summer tide. Reluctantly, Nora returned to party dresses and china patterns and the thieving lies of wayward brothers as she waited for another crumb from the old woman.

———————

Gordon taught Rose to drive. Each night they cruised into town long after the single stoplight had been turned off, blinking an endless yellow in their direction. Gordon found the school bus barn, and it was as if they had tapped an oil well. They filled all their gas cans and a half-dozen milk jugs besides. He taught Rose how to hold the hose in her mouth and suck just until she felt the pressure, the slight tang of fumes on her tongue. Gordon had a habit, Rose observed, of

< 214 >

appearing to be looking straight ahead while, in fact, he was watching everything to the side of him. Twice he had put his hand on the inside of her thigh as they drove, shrugging only slightly when she removed it, as if he'd hardly noticed that his hand had strayed. He tried to kiss her once, too, awkwardly, gasoline still on their tongues. Rose pushed him away, spitting into the weeds, and they had gone right back to their sibling alliance. For all his height, Gordon was skinny and weak.

In the Maverick, they found a world entirely separate from the daytime. In the Maverick, everything belonged to them alone. They drove down the beach access roads. They plowed through the empty sand, rumbling over the high tide line on Gold Egg Beach. They discovered the shadows of logging roads. On a moonlit night, from the top of a logging bluff, Rose spun the car to a stop and pointed out her father's island to Gordon.

"Car crash, I heard," Gordon said, giving her one of those sidelong looks.

Rose opened her mouth to answer, but she was speechless, staring at the far-off hazy hump of her father's island beyond the black water.

---

Nora lost more weight. Her skin seemed thinner, too, translucent and delicate. Mrs. Falcon sent over cream scones that nearly broke Rose's teeth and a Lady Baltimore cake that reeked of mouthwash.

"Tell your mother she needs to eat," was the message Mrs. Falcon sent to Rose through Gordon. But Rose could stand directly in front of Nora, practically screaming, and her mother would not leave her trance. Gordon played drums on the kitchen pots; the cats yowled from inattention. Nora moved upstairs to the armchair in her bedroom. The only one who seemed to hold her attention was the old witch, Winckett, the rest home pretender from the island.

Old Winckett was, so she said, a distant cousin of Eddie's grandfather. A cousin then, but she did not have any Eddie in her that Rose could see. In Rose's father's photographs, the Marvels were all fair-haired and freckled, with sensitive eyes that resulted in a squint by the time they reached their thirties. They had long thin faces and pretty mouths with slight overbites and children's pearl teeth. Winckett was a dark little woman, her face scrunched together. Woven within her white hair were strands of black that glistened as if she oiled them. Black hairs grew between her eyebrows, out of a mole on the left side of her face, and in a thin line above her upper lip. Her narrow, pinched lips were cracked, and the corners ran continually with saliva that she dabbed at with a soiled handkerchief. She reminded Rose of an ancient, cunning monkey. She claimed to know about an old family homestead, still intact. She could draw a map, she said. But she never did. Instead, she spooled out stories.

"You know these, girl," she sing-songed at Nora, "you'll know the island, all the secret family places a fellow might choose to hide."

Strangely, that seemed enough for Nora, who had treated Eddie's agitation those last weeks with a frustration that now seemed to shame her. All he needed was time, she seemed to have concluded, time to heal and regroup.

On their way to the Mary Flower Home, Nora always stopped at Closet Creek Carry-Out to purchase treats for Winckett. She called this the Price of Admission. Nora, who had never allowed Rose to spend her own pocket money on a single chocolate toffee, now filled a shopping bag with treats wrapped in dusty cellophane. It was all the old woman seemed to eat. Her love for chocolate stained the rheumy corners of her mouth and gave her a greedy, alert expression. She hoarded Nora's gifts in her beside drawer, nibbling at whatever her hand touched until the ants got in, and then she railed at the staff who cleared away the mess, vacuuming the ants without a single word

< 216 >

of reproach. Rose peered into the drawer once, and she told Gordon later how she saw stiff cakes the color of dried mud; long chocolate biscuits gone white at the edges; and musty-smelling chocolate straws that she had seen only in Canada on a trip with her grandfather years ago. The old woman had picked and gnawed on every article in the drawer as if marking each for her alone. Rose thought they looked like animal droppings.

Lacey Dorchester, Mary Flower's social director, shook her head once when they were leaving, when Winckett called Nora back to wait on her one more time.

"Poor woman," Lacey said, drawing Rose aside. "You should make her stay home. You know, don't you, that your daddy's dead?"

Rose nodded, although until that moment she wasn't sure entirely that she did believe he was gone for good. Her mother's quest, her faith, had borne them past their initial hard grief. For the first time in months, as she watched her mother cradle the old woman with one arm, helping her down the hall, Rose felt her chest heave involuntarily under the weight of missing her father. Right after the accident, she had cried all the time, even waking from dreams to find her cheeks wet and her eyes sore.

"She's not related to Dad," she told Nora in the truck as they drove home.

"Look at me, Mommy." Rose shook her mother's arm and the truck bounced toward the shoulder. "If he were there, he'd let us know."

Nora barely turned her head toward Rose as she righted the wheel.

The next week Rose left her mother in the truck as they were leaving, on the pretense of needing the bathroom. Her mother was in a daze, trying to piece together a Winckett story of Eddie's first boat—fir planks tied together with strands of cedar bark.

Rose found the old woman in her room, sorting out her chocolates.

"Leave her alone," she whispered fiercely.

In a voice unlike the island cadence she presented to Nora, Mrs. Winckett hissed at Rose like an ancient gangster.

"Get lost," she said. "Take a hike."

"You're hurting her."

"Go jump a cliff," the old woman stuttered with a smile that showed off her ruined teeth.

A madwoman. And outside, her mother in tears, clutching the steering wheel of her father's unmoving truck.

———

"Why doesn't your mom just go there and see for herself?" Gordon asked. His grandmother was so intent on her latest project—her masterpiece, she called it—that she was still up, well past her nine o'clock bedtime, and the children were housebound. Rose got a brief glimpse of Mrs. Falcon throwing cups of high-rising flour into an enormous yellow mixing bowl.

"Someone will die from that cake," Gordon pronounced, catching the expression on Rose's face as Mrs. Falcon drizzled a thin green stream of what looked like antifreeze into her batter.

They moved to the screened porch and listened to Claudine Falcon's mixer screeching in the kitchen.

"She can't," Rose said. "She gets too sick. She's already sick."

"We could go. You don't get sick, do you? *I'll* go."

"You'd go anywhere."

"I would," Gordon admitted. "How hard can it be to find a boat to borrow?"

Rose smiled in spite of herself. The Maverick's back floor was piled with items "borrowed" from unlocked cars in Salish Bay—tapes and sweatshirts, a bottle opener with a *Go Cougars!* logo on it. She shook her head. "No, I won't. He's not there. Besides," she added, "my mother wouldn't believe me. The only one she listens to is Winckett—the pig."

Gordon leaned forward in his seat to light a joint. The screen porch filled with an aroma that reminded Rose of moss and damp fur. Gordon's teeth glistened as he bared them in a smile, smoke escaping in thin streams. Rose could feel his excitement.

"How's this," he said, sipping the air as he inhaled, "for a plan?"

———————

Eleven o'clock on an April evening, Rose eases her bedroom door closed behind her. Her mother is asleep in the next room, worn out from Winckett's teasing, her face on the pillow golden in the hall light she keeps burning like her own heart, steady and lonesome. Rose hugs the edges of the stairs so that the wood doesn't sing her presence. Out the kitchen door, into the damp night, the funneled wind. New leaves and thin branches flung across the gravel drive that separates these two furthermost houses on Little River Road, the outpost of Salish Bay. And here is Gordon, waiting beside the barn under the madrona trees whose discarded shivers of red bark curl like tiny wounds over the silver Maverick, the car Gordon has already shifted into neutral. Then the two of them push through the gravel, their light footsteps hidden beneath the wind. Away from those two lonely houses to the blacktop of Little River Road, the black road, the empty road, where soon they're running, the doors half open. Rose will drive this time. Watch how she slips so easily behind the wheel while Gordon, with a well-practiced jump, lands one foot onto the doorjamb before ducking inside himself. A routine, anyone could see at a glance, performed each night in stealth because they are children after all. Gordon is fourteen and Rose a half-year younger. How else could they fly if not in the ever-trilling dark, the engine silent until they are out of earshot, already lost?

Eleven o'clock. Not so late, but late enough for a secluded edge of town, populated only by two widow women and a pair of children. All along the coast that night, travelers' advisories are calling people home, but for the two children, especially Rose, the weather is a familiar, as if all their wild longings have pushed beyond their meager bodies into the world which can itself barely contain them. Rose turns the radio on to its fullest volume to match the rhythms she hears outside and smiles as the Maverick rocks like a foolish ship alone in the storm. Gordon nudges her and, ignorant of any real danger, passes her a newly lit joint. But Rose knows. In the rearview mirror, tree limbs swoon across the road behind them like calls to their blind backs. The children smoke, their faces briefly illuminated. They push through the tearing wind and the wretched, receiving night to the bridge where the river is rising and past there to the cliff road, the old logging trail, all Rose's choices this night. Just as the Maverick begins to buck the potholes and gravel and jutting roots of that upward trail, the rain slams down upon them, blinding the children under its racketing. Rose forges ahead, trusting the Maverick to keep to the gravel, to beat through the fingers of tree boughs, whisking across the side windows. Gordon's eyes are closed—under the tumult, he's humming like crazy.

Storms come and go. They are of no importance to Rose. The Maverick rises steadily up the logging road into the eerie light of a besieged night sky. Abruptly, the narrow road curves to the right and the Maverick miraculously follows, the storm beating on its back, down the road that is almost a trail, that crosses another rough bridge and, still climbing, meets the lonely pavement of the county road.

In Dahline, the storm has passed. The Mary Flower Home is almost dark. A single center room, the nurses' station, illuminated. Rose points out Winckett's room on the northernmost corner, entangled by the fiercest of the climbing roses. Gordon reaches into the back of the Maverick and carefully removes the tall box that he has taken from his grandmother's kitchen.

If the aides who catalog the night at Mary Flower choose this time to check on Winckett, they might think they are dreaming. Rose does, and she knows better. She stands outside the window in the open space Gordon has made with his buck knife among the tangled, thorny canes and watches as Gordon's shadowy figure unveils Mrs. Falcon's latest, a seven-layer devil's food wedding cake. There is only one figure atop the cake. Gordon had insisted on one and Rose plucked the first she could find, the little plastic cougar that sat on her dresser. Her father once told her that cougars are called the ghosts of the forests since they move so stealthily. For Rose, this seems a fitting representation of old Winckett: treacherous, craving, dead.

Gordon finds Mrs. Winckett's little bedside lamp, and her eyes glow greedily in the semi-darkened room when she sees what he has brought her. It's no surprise to Rose how the old woman accepts Gordon's offering so easily. She's a taker, the old woman is. Rose watches Gordon from the window; it's as if he and Winckett are on stage. She observes as he pulls a spoon from the pocket of his jeans and wheels the cake on the bedside trolley so close to the old woman her hands begin to twitch. For what seems like an hour, Gordon feeds Winckett. Her ugly mouth opens again and again in anticipation. Rose can hear her grunts, her heightened breath growing steadily weaker, melding into the night sounds around her—the click of crickets, the echo of a barking dog, old rain shuffling through leaves.

While she waits for Gordon to finish, Rose remembers a story her father told about another game ravens play. A grieving ritual, he thought. Huddled on treetops, they'll watch solemnly while one of their own lofts himself into the air, higher and higher, higher and higher, before suddenly, without warning, he loses all that lovely upward drift and begins to plummet. What had been grace ascending a mere moment before now becomes a fast-falling dead weight. Is he hurt? Is he dead? If not, surely he will be when the ground smacks against him. The trees have never been so quiet. Even the wind ceases its useless twirling. And oh how time stretches! What should take a moment, an instant you'd miss if you merely glanced away, is endless. Little raven hearts nearly burst from the pressure of anticipation.

And so the raven falls. Backwards, its great wings spread wide. Like a rock. Like a hurled weight. The ravens left in the tree begin to jostle one another, a rapid jittering that breaks the silence. Squawks of raucous glee erupt as the raven falls and falls. From every branch, they offer encouragement to the plummeting bird, the rock, the weight, which at the very last minute comes alive, flipping and bouncing onto the wind. Wings flapping easily, our hero shoots back to the tree's crown, where the other ravens greet him with more squawks and full, almost intelligible words. Wings overlap wings in good will as they push each other toward the edge of a bough.

*Who's next? Who's next?*

The old woman will die, Rose knows, her witch's heart stopped by greed, and when in the morning Rose's mother hears the news, she will understand finally what Rose is learning: that death can't be called back; that it comes unbidden, however much we hide ourselves, no matter how far we are from home. Those behind can only keep up the pretense—*catch, release, catch, release*—until the game is over.

# ACKNOWLEDGMENTS

I am grateful to the editors of the journals where many of these stories, in slightly altered forms, first appeared:

*Blackbird*, "Two Girls Off Quarry Road"
*Cincinnati Review*, "Temptation of the Tutelary"
*Colorado Review*, "Pearl-Diving"
*Fiction Southeast*, "Pink Cloud"
*Narrative Magazine*, "The New Arrival," "Swallow"
*Ontario Review*, "The Farmhouse Wife"
*The Sun*, "Lost in the War of the Beautiful Lads"
*Willow Springs*, "Catch, Release"

I am also deeply indebted to Rick Barot, the Civitella Ranieri Foundation, Dana Prescott, and the intensely talented and generous company of artists and writers I found there. I wish they were all still just down the ghostly castle hall. These stories have been enriched, too, by Judy Sternlight's steady, brilliant, and kind friendship and the great Debra Magpie Earling's magical and loving wisdom. The late and much-missed Judith Kitchen put me on my way again when I floundered early on, and I wish she could see the whole of where she led me. And the extraordinary Duncan Scovil remains my most valued reader and creative instigator.

Finally, I owe more than I can say to Wyatt Prunty and the sustaining, ever-inspiring and generous Sewanee community.

< 223 >

## FICTION TITLES IN THE SERIES